HEXAGON STAR QUILTS

The colorful star network on the Star Chart quilt (see page 65) was appliquéd.

HEXAGON STAR QUILTS

113 English Paper-Pieced Star Patterns to Piece and Appliqué

CATHY PERLMUTTER

Landauer Publishing

For Alan, Eli, and Riva, my stars.

Hexagon Star Quilts

Landauer Publishing, *www.landauerpub.com*, is an imprint of Fox Chapel Publishing Company, Inc.

Project Team
Acquisition Editor: Tiffany Hill
Editor: Katie Ocasio
Copy Editor: Amy Deputato
Designer: Wendy Reynolds
Indexer: Jay Kreider
Photographers: Mike Mihalo, Sue Voegtlin, and Cathy Perlmutter

ISBN 978-1-947163-35-5

Library of Congress Cataloging-in-Publication Data

Names: Perlmutter, Cathy, 1957– author.
Title: Hexagon star quilts / Cathy Perlmutter.
Description: Mount Joy : Landauer Publishing, [2020] | Includes
   index. | Summary: "Instructs quilters on English paper piecing
   supplies and techniques to create hexagon star quilts. Also
   includes several projects and over 100 hexagon star patterns"—
   Provided by publisher.
Identifiers: LCCN 2019054797 (print) | LCCN 201905498 (ebook)
   | ISBN 9781947163355 (paperback) | ISBN 9781607657989
   (ebook)
Subjects: LCSH: Patchwork—Patterns. | Quilting—Patterns. | Star
   quilts. | Hexagons—Miscellanea.
Classification: LCC TT835 .P35219 2020 (print) | LCC TT835
   (ebook) | DDC 746.46/041—dc23
LC record available at https://lccn.loc.gov/2019054797
LC ebook record available at https://lccn.loc.gov/2019054798

We are always looking for talented authors.
To submit an idea, please send a brief inquiry to
acquisitions@foxchapelpublishing.com.

Printed in China
Second printing

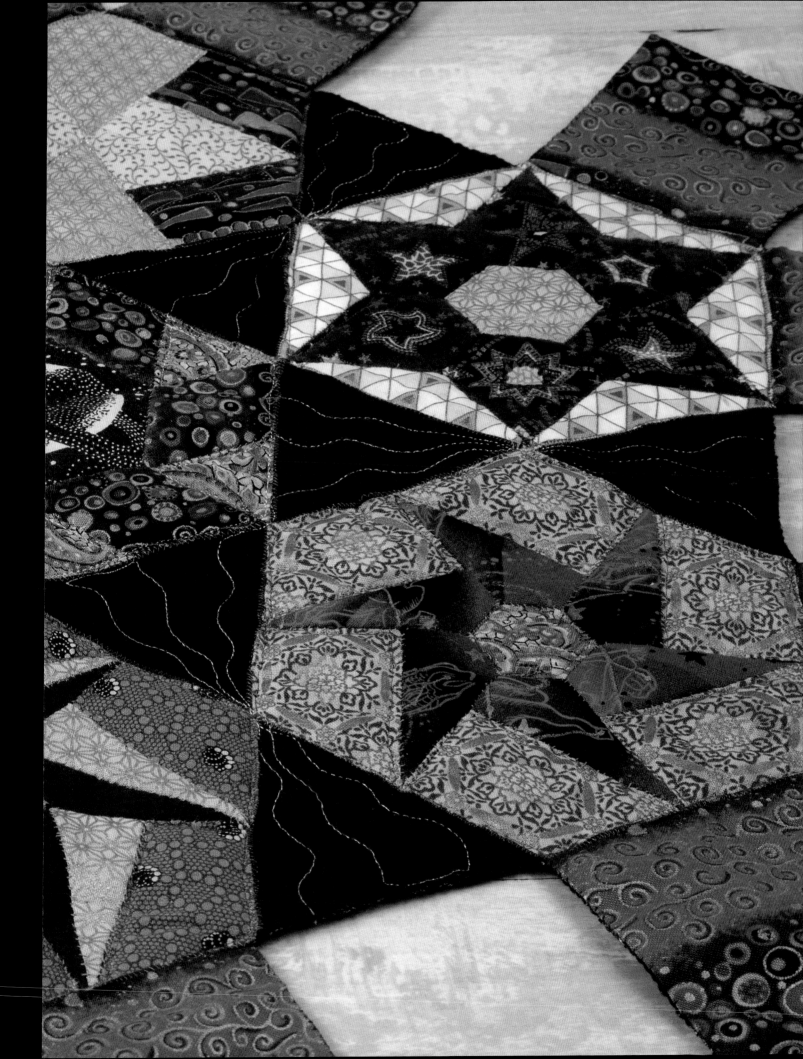

Contents

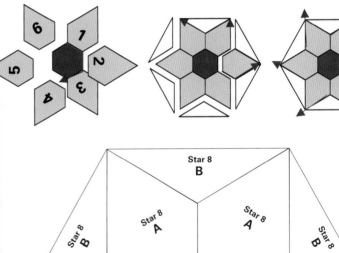

Everyone Loves Stars!

Quilted stars are beautiful and impressive, but piecing them can be quite a challenge. Conventional piecing requires precision, and Y seams are an ordeal.

That's where English paper piecing, or EPP, comes in. This eighteenth-century British technique makes creating stars much easier. There's less math, and Y seams are a breeze. Imperfect seam allowances are a nonissue.

And even if you want to pin, you can't!

Throughout this book, I'll feature stars inside hexagons. Hexagons and other shapes made up of 60-degee angles create fascinating optical illusions of depth, and they fit together in wondrous ways.

How to Use This Book

This book is an excellent resource for all quilters, regardless of their experience and skill level in EPP. Newcomers to EPP will find a wealth of information needed to begin to learn the craft. The project on page 46 is an easy first EPP project that will leave you excited for more. More experienced EPP quilters will be able to build their knowledge of the craft, and use the star patterns I provide (starting on page 74) for future quilt projects. Quilt teachers will find this book a great way to teach their students the fundamentals of EPP and how to create vivid hexagon star projects.

When copied and printed, each hexagon in this book measures 6" (15.25cm) across from tip to opposite tip and each side is 3" (7.6cm). If you like, you can increase the size, but I wouldn't make them smaller because some stars already have tiny pieces. All of the hexagon patterns have been numbered from 1 to 113 (see pages 74–130) and are referred to this way throughout the book.

There are seven projects in the book (see page 45), and there's also information to help you design your own project (see page 138). A single finished block can be appliquéd to make a place mat, tote bag, pillow, sweatshirt, or the like. Groups can be appliquéd or pieced with other stars and shapes to make quilts of all sizes. You can work on a quilt as a group project with your quilting group or some friends, each making a few stars to add to the finished project.

If you're new to EPP, start with the simpler stars that have relatively few, large pieces. Work your way up to the more complex stars. With each block you create, you'll strengthen your EPP skills. The stars below demonstrate the difficulty levels of the stars in this book, from easy to complex. The simple star (on the far left) has six pieces to cut and sew together, the intermediate star (in the middle) has thirteen pieces, and the difficult star (on the far right) has twenty-four pieces.

From left to right:
Star 1, page 74;
Star 10, page 78;
Star 95, page 121.

English Paper Piecing Supplies

Here are some basic supplies for EPP. Even though I share the brands I use, you can always switch them out for others you may prefer.

- **Thread:** When doing EPP by hand, I usually use a medium value neutral-color thread, like gray. For hand sewing, any strong, quality thread will work, but I especially like Superior Threads Bottom Line or Wonderfil Invisafil™, which are thin, don't twist, and knot less than regular thread.

  For machine sewing, I also like Bottom Line or InvisaFil™. You can also choose "invisible" polyester or nylon monofilament thread; it shows the least, but does create a shine. Bobbin thread should match the color of the top thread or the fabric. If you put "invisible" thread in a bobbin, wind it no more than halfway—otherwise, it can break bobbins. If you want to advertise the stitching, use a decorative thread and stitch.

- **Glue stick or pen:** Glue pens are found in the notions or quilting section of fabric stores (and online, of course). There are several different brands—the one in the photo is my Fons & Porter pen—but they all work the same way. These pen-sized devices hold a small tube-shaped cartridge of glue. The tip is significantly narrower than a regular glue stick—only about a ¼" (0.64cm) across. That means when you use a pen to apply glue, much less of it will wind up where you don't want it, such as on your table, ironing board, cardstock, or fingers.

  You only have to buy the pen once (it runs around $10), but you will go through glue cartridges pretty quickly. The cartridges—each is it its own lidded plastic container—run around $1.50–$3.00 each. For a large quilt, you're going to need lots of them, so buy a multi-pack! I like using my glue pen when I'm travelling, because there's less mess and less need for hand wipes.

  A regular school glue stick is less expensive and holds everything down just as well as the glue pen, but more of the glue will go where you don't want. So, with a regular stick, it's a good idea to lay down a piece of parchment paper or other protection for the table or ironing board underneath the fabric and cardstock template you're basting.

  Although there's more glue in a stick than in a pen cartridge, if you're embarking on a large project, you should still buy a pack of a half-dozen school glue sticks to start with—they disappear more quickly than you may think.

- **Cardstock printer paper:** To print templates, standard 65-lb. cardstock works fine. If your printer won't take cardstock, print the pattern onto paper and glue the paper to cardstock (see description on page 13).

- **Slender, strong hand-sewing needles:** I tend to grab any slender needle that's handy. My favorite for EPP is Hemmings size 11 milliners.

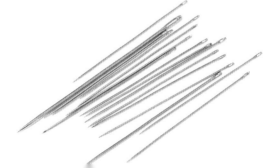

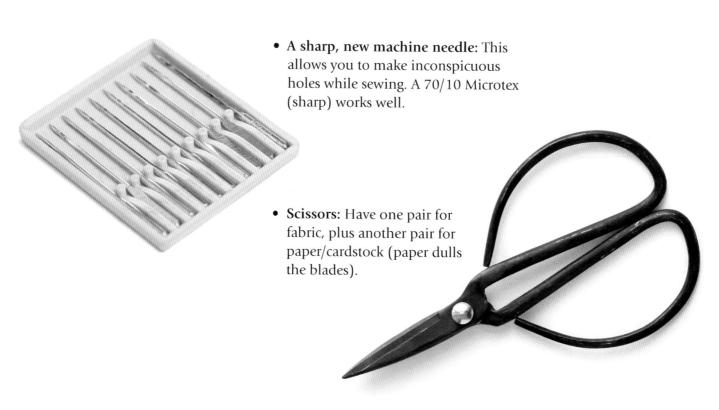

- **A sharp, new machine needle:** This allows you to make inconspicuous holes while sewing. A 70/10 Microtex (sharp) works well.

- **Scissors:** Have one pair for fabric, plus another pair for paper/cardstock (paper dulls the blades).

- **Embossing stylus:** It's not mandatory, but this pencil-sized tool (below) does a great job breaking through glue on cardstock template and prying them out, with minimal risk of poking through fabric. The ball should be at least ⅝" to ¾" (1.5 to 2cm). The one I use is from the Royal & Langnickel Brush Embossing Set, and something similar is in the Artminds™ Embossing Stylus Tool Set. Use a plumper end.

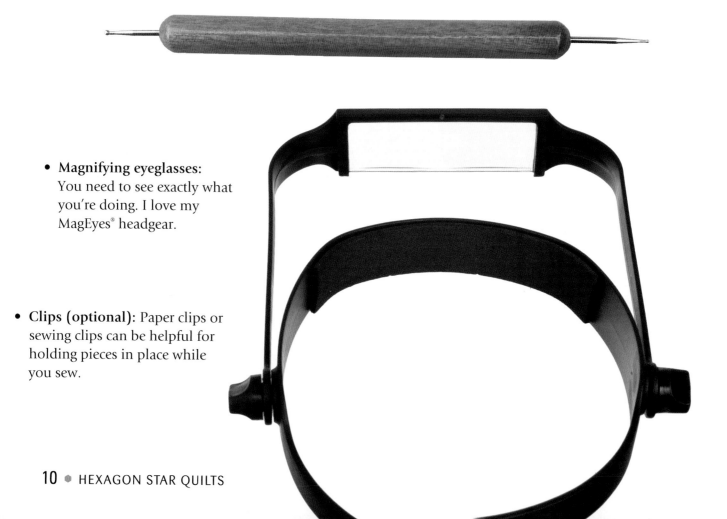

- **Magnifying eyeglasses:** You need to see exactly what you're doing. I love my MagEyes® headgear.

- **Clips (optional):** Paper clips or sewing clips can be helpful for holding pieces in place while you sew.

- **Quality sewing machine and high-visibility zigzag foot:** Your machine should function well at slow speeds. The zigzag stitch should be reliable (no skips), and it should handle monofilament thread in the bobbin and top if that's the thread you like. The foot should also give you a clear view of the edges running underneath it (I prefer an open-toe appliqué foot). If you don't have all of these things, your blocks may wind up a mess. Trust me—I know this from experience.

- **Thread Conditioner:** Reduces spontaneous thread knotting. There are several types; find them in the notions section of a sewing store (and online). I use a beeswax conditioner with a plastic casing that has slots to send the thread through. Other styles and brands I recommend are Sew Fine Thread Gloss™ and Thread Magic™.

- **Awl:** This item is also called a "needle-pointed hobby awl." Mine is metal and pencil sized. It helps arrange and rearrange tails as blocks move through the machine.

- **Tweezers or a curved hemostat:** Optional; I sometimes need these to pull cardstock templates out of sharp points and other reluctant regions. A long curved hemostat is ideal.

- **Décor Bond® interfacing:** Optional; for machine EPP only. It stays in place permanently. If you go this route, you won't need to pull out templates, you don't need the hemostat or embossing stylus, and you can sew with a longer stitch.

English Paper Piecing

Once you have the basic supplies, you can begin planning your project and creating your stars. Pick a star and then copy and print the page you want directly onto cardstock via your printer (Option A). If your printer does not take cardstock, see Option B; for those with pigment-ink printers, see Option C.

Option A: Print Directly to Cardstock

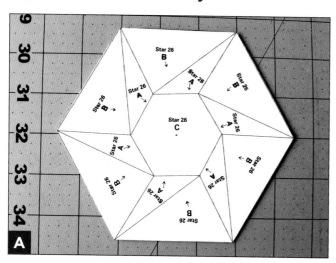

1. If you're using a printed copy of the book, scan the pattern and print it out onto cardstock, or photocopy it onto cardstock (A). If you're printing from a digital copy of this book and your printer menu lets you change the setting to heavy paper or cardstock, try that, but the patterns may print out fine on a normal setting. If you're using a printed copy of the book, photocopy the patterns onto cardstock. After you've printed each star pattern, measure the outer hexagon; it should be 6" (15.25cm) from one corner to the opposite corner and 3" (7.6cm) per flat side. If not, check the print menu to be sure it's printing at full size.

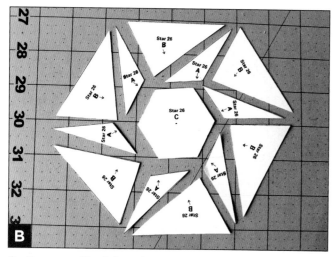

2. Cut out all of the pieces on the lines (B).

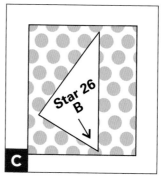
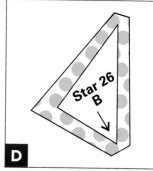

3. Place each cardstock piece onto the BACK of the fabric, with markings facing up so you can read them throughout the piecing process (C).

4. Cut the fabric about ⅜" to ½" (0.95 to 1.3cm) larger all the way around (D). Absolute precision is NOT required here!

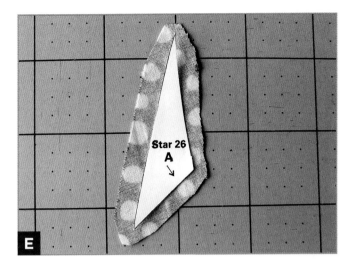

5. If it's a tiny triangle or has narrow sharp points, cut a little less of a seam allowance (just under ¼" [0.65cm]). You can also cut straight across, a scant ¼" (0.65cm) above the cardstock triangle's tips (E). You may want to "fussy-cut" your fabrics. Refer to page 16.

6. When you've done all of these steps, it's time to baste. See page 17.

Option B: Print on Paper and Glue to Cardstock

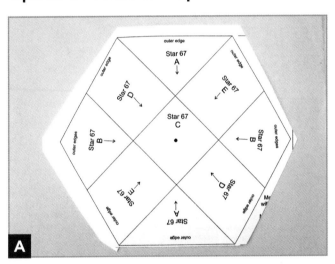

1. If your printer does not take cardstock, photocopy and print the page onto copy paper. Check that the hexagon is 6" (15.25cm) from corner to opposite corner and 3" (7.6cm) per flat side. If not, check that the printer is printing at full size.

2. Rough-cut around the pattern, outside the boundaries (A).

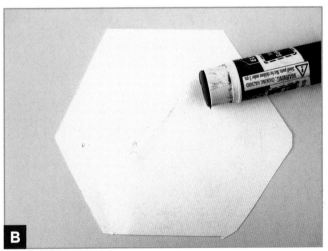

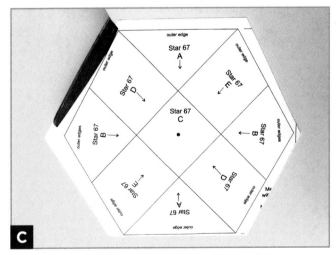

3. Use a glue stick lightly over the back and then press the pattern to the cardstock (I used an old manila file folder) (B). Let the glue dry.

4. Cut out all of the shapes on the lines (C).

5. Follow steps 3 to 5 under Option A.

Option C: Print on Décor Bond

Décor Bond 809®, by Pellon, sold by the yard, is an inexpensive medium-heavy interfacing with fusible glue on one side. It doesn't shrink with heat or pressure. The huge advantage is that it stays in place permanently, so after machine sewing, you won't face the problems that ripping out cardstock can cause.

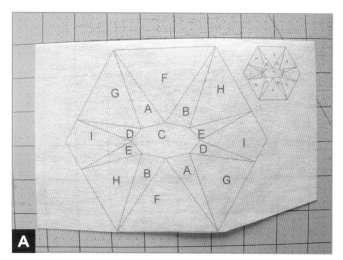

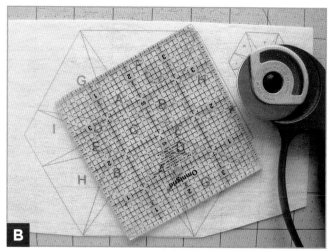

1. FOR PIGMENT-INK PRINTERS ONLY: Pigment inks are water resistant. Dye-based printer inks may smear on the fabric. Your printer manual will tell you what kind of ink it is, or do a simple test—drip some water on a paper printout, and if it doesn't smear, you probably have pigment ink. If you're using a pigment-ink printer, cut the Décor Bond into 8½" x 11" (216 x 280mm) sheets, and then run the sheet through your printer, printing on the non-glue side (A). If you don't have a printer that uses pigment ink, do the next step instead.

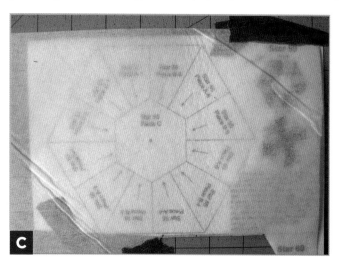

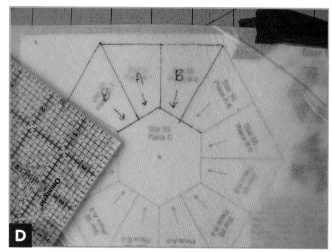

2. Print or photocopy the star pattern onto paper first and then tape it to a surface (C). Tape Décor Bond on top, shiny/glue side down. Use a fine-point permanent marker and small ruler to trace lines accurately (D). Copy the arrows and letters on each Décor Bond piece (D).

3. The next step, whether you've printed or traced your patterns, is to cut out each Décor Bond piece (B and D; you can use scissors, or a rotary cutter and small ruler). Press them onto the back of the fabric, using a wool setting with steam. Don't scrub the iron, or you might distort the pattern pieces. Instead, pick the iron up and put it down.

4. Cut out each fabric piece ⅜" to ½" (0.95 to 1.3cm) larger than the template (E).

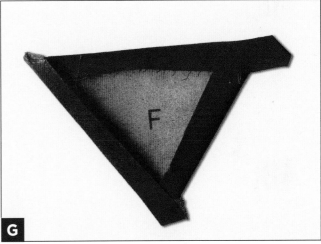

5. Fold the edges in (F and G), relying on your fingertips to fold accurately over small points. A little bit of glue in corners helps hold things in place.

How to Fussy-Cut

Fussy-cutting—when fabric is cut to feature part of a print, and several pieces need to be identical—can create stunning kaleidoscopic effects in your hexagon stars.

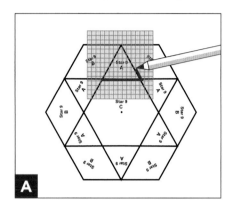

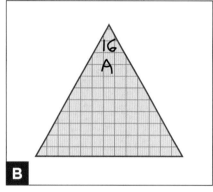

1. Print a star pattern onto paper or cardstock. Trace the piece you want to fussy-cut onto template plastic, gridded or un-gridded (A). I prefer gridded.

2. Cut out the template. Jot the star number and piece letter on it (B).

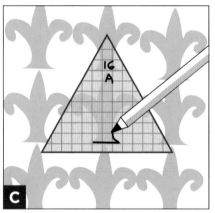

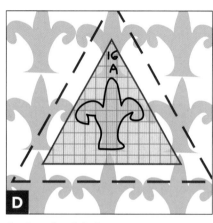

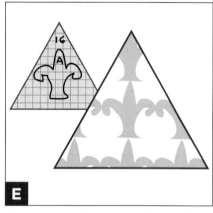

3. Slide it around the fabric until you find a location you like (C). Trace a few lines from the print with a pencil (so you can erase and reuse it later.) With gridded plastic, it's helpful to center the midline in the design's center.

4. Cut the fabric ½" (1.3cm) from the template edges (or ¼" [0.65cm] out for a tiny piece). Draw the cutting line (the red dashed line above) and use scissors or a rotary cutter on a flat surface (D).

5. Now you have your first fabric piece, which will be larger than the template (E).

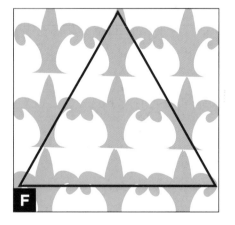

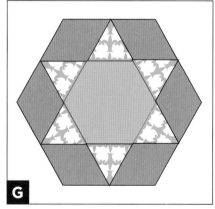

6. Place the first piece back on the fabric. Slide it around until you find the same formation (F). Pin it in place and cut close around it. Repeat for all of the pieces needed (usually three or six). Baste them to cardstock or use Décor Bond (see pages 14–15).

7. Here's how these points will look in the block (G).

How to Baste a Shape

In English paper piecing, there are many ways to baste, but they all boil down to the same thing: folding fabric edges tightly around a stiff shape, with corner folds that all point in the same direction.

Method #1: Glue Stick or Glue Pen

Gluing is *much* faster than hand basting, and I think it's more accurate. At home, I usually use a regular school glue stick (purple or white). For tiny pieces, and on the road, I use a glue pen. If you both glue AND iron, it's even easier and faster.

Method #2: Needle and Thread

This is the traditional method. Take long running stitches through the seam allowances around each shape. Don't penetrate the cardstock. Pull the thread tight to bring in the edges. At each corner, take a tacking stitch. This method is very portable, but it's slow and tricky with tiny shapes.

Running stitch on a hexagon

Running stitch on a square

Apply starch with a small paintbrush.

Method #3: Starch Basting

Spray a little starch or sizing into a shallow dish (I usually use a plastic lid as a dish). With a small paintbrush, paint it onto the cut-out fabric piece just outside the cardstock shape. Wait a moment for the starch or sizing to spread, and then press seam allowances inward. The disadvantage is that the templates may slip out before you want them to. If your printer ink isn't waterproof, the starch may smear the print on the templates, so test the printouts with a few drops of water first. If it smears, don't use this technique. You don't want the ink to leach onto your fabrics.

Method #4: Décor Bond (and Glue Stick), for Machine EPPers

As explained earlier, Décor Bond 809® by Pellon has advantages, most notably that you never rip it out. However, because it's not as stiff or thick as cardstock, it does make it a little harder to baste accurately. Use a gentle touch—you'll get better at feeling edges and folding fabric over them. See page 14 for instructions on using Décor Bond.

Baste with Commitment and Consistency

When I started EPPing, I didn't pay much attention to the advice that my corner folds should all point in the same direction. I was too busy figuring out everything else! When it came time to join pieces, however, I quickly learned that within the same project, you MUST be consistent about which edge of each corner you turn in first. If not, the shape may be distorted, and the seam allowances may collide with one another, making a neat fit difficult to impossible.

Still confused? We'll work through it with an example.

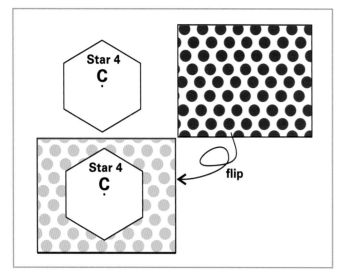

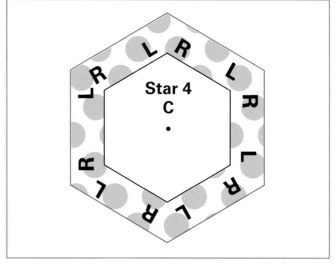

Let's say you've cut out a hexagon template, piece C. The fabric is a red polka-dot fabric, where the right side of the fabric is vivid and the wrong side is paler.

Rough-cut the fabric about ½" (1.3cm) out from all template sides (go down to a generous ¼" [0.65cm] for sharp, small triangles and points). Imagine that there are "L" and "R" markings at each corner, indicating its left and the right sides.

Fold in one side of each corner at a time. Here's where you'll make a MONUMENTAL commitment: do you fold in the LEFT side first, or the RIGHT side first? When I started making projects for this book, I decided to always fold the left corner in first, for no particular reason. If you prefer the opposite, follow the same procedure but turn the shape clockwise as you go. Whichever you choose, stick with it, not only for each entire block, but also for the entire project that you're planning to stitch the blocks into. Yes, this might even turn into a lifetime commitment!

> For all of the projects in this book, place the template on the back of the fabric, with the printed side of the cardstock facing up at you.

Hexagons

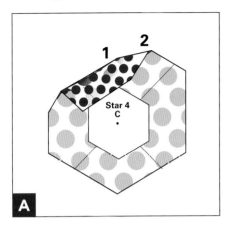

A

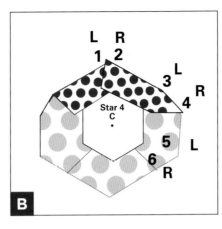

B

1. Start at the top corner (A). Fold the left side of the corner in. A dab of glue under the flap will help hold it. Put a dab of glue on top.

2. Next, fold in at corner 2, the right side of the corner, and press (B). At this point, I rotate the piece counterclockwise so corners 3 and 4 are at the top (not shown).

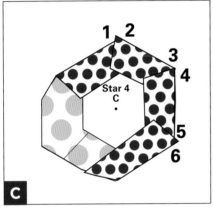

C

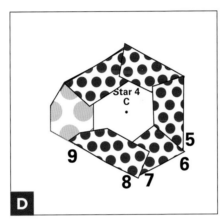

D

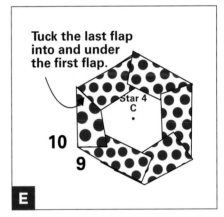

E

3. Fold in corner 3. Dab glue on top, and fold in corner 4. Continue to do corners 5 and 6, 7 and 8, and 9 and 10 (C to E).

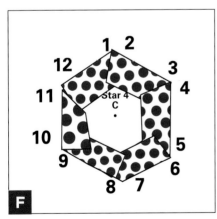

F

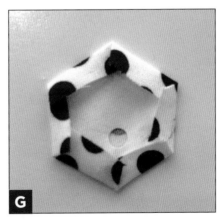

G

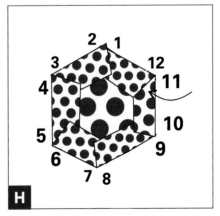

H

4. For that last corner flap (number 11), tuck the seam allowance into and under the seam allowance between corners 11 and 12 (F). Notice how all of the folds are pointing counterclockwise.

5. This is what a hexagon basted this way will look like from the back (G).

6. This diagram shows how the finished piece would look with right sides folded in first. Notice how all of the folds are pointing clockwise (H).

Angular Shapes

With triangles and other shapes with sharp angles, it's easier to see why you must stick with one folding direction. Folding sharp angles generates what EPPers call "tails," "flags," or "dog ears."

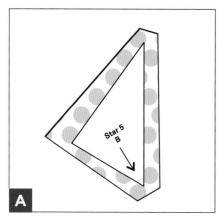

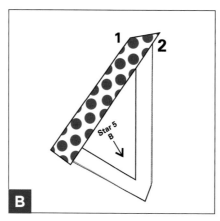

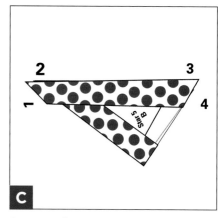

1. Starting at the top, fold the left side of the top corner over to the right, at 1. Push side 2 over to the left, making a crease in flap 1 (A and B).

2. Turn the piece counter-clockwise 90 degrees (C). Push down corner 3.

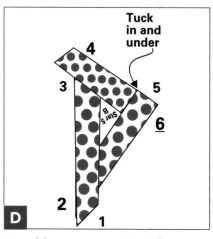

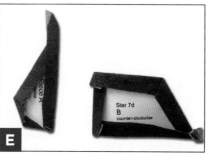

4. Take a look at these oddly shaped pieces. They're all folded the same way, with the tails pointing counterclockwise when viewed from the back (E). The second photo (F) shows the same pieces from the front—from this perspective, the tails point clockwise.

3. Fold corner 4 to the left. Rotate 90 degrees again. Fold corner 5 into and underneath flap 6 (D). Glue and, if you're at the ironing board, press well.

5. Here's an equilateral triangle, front and back, with its three flags pointing in the same direction, counterclockwise from the back (G) and clockwise from the front (H).

Why Worry about Consistency?

You may think that this is all a bit compulsive. But when you start putting pieces together, you'll be glad you did it. The seam allowances will nest underneath each other, making it easier to sew pieces together. For example, in the two photos of the red-and-white basted pieces, the seam allowances on both triangles point clockwise (from the front). Their tails will slide underneath each other, allowing them to fit snugly against one another (A and B).

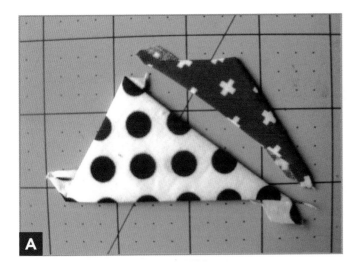

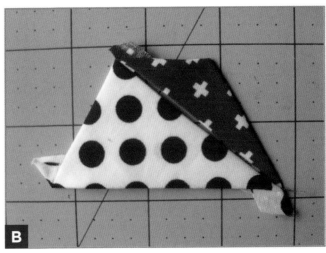

In the back view of the star block (C), you can see how consistent pressing of seam allowances creates a neat whirl in the middle. Along the outer edge, the gold bar and blue triangle tails also nest together.

After you've finished basting, it's time to piece the block together!

Piecing Order

In English paper piecing, stitch order is forgiving. If you apply common sense, it's hard to go wrong, but some routes are more efficient. Piecing suggestions are in each block description, and here are some basic concepts, but feel free to try it your way.

3+3 Stars

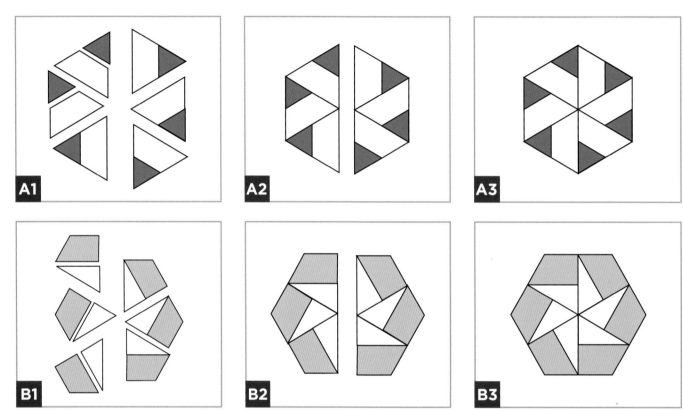

In these blocks (Star 12 on page 79 and Star 18 on page 82), six tips meet in the middle. It's best to start by creating six wedges that may be triangular or diamond-shaped. The pieces within each wedge are joined first (A1 and B1). Next, three wedges are sewn into a half-block. Sew three more together to make the other half (A2 and B2). Finally, join halves along their midline (A3 and B3). When hand sewing, I like to sew that last seam from the center out, in both directions, to maximize accuracy. When machine sewing, I stitch from one end to the other.

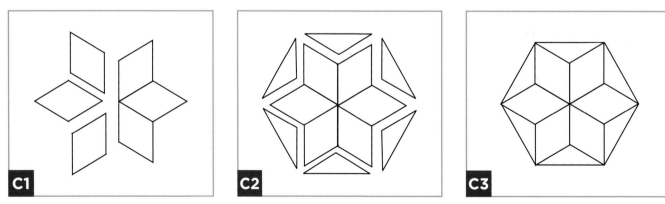

In some blocks, the process is slightly different. The first step will be to make the two halves of the interior pattern (C1), and then sew them together. The last step is to inset pieces around the edges, like the wide triangles inset into the diamond shapes (C2 and C3). (See Star 7 on page 77 for the block above.)

Centerpiece Stars

If there's a piece in the center—usually a hexagon, but sometimes another shape—attach pieces consecutively around it (A1, B1, and C1). You can go all the way around without cutting thread. When hand sewing, I do loop knots at the end of each piece.

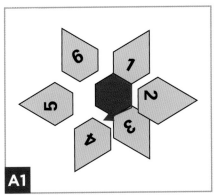

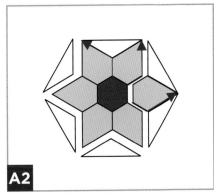

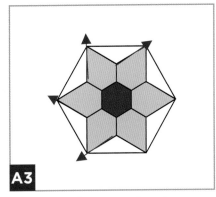

Once the pieces surrounding the center are attached, stitch outward along the seams between the pieces (for example, the short seams between pieces 1 to 6 in A1). You may then stitch one edge of a background piece, shown in A2. All that remains in this case is to sew the final background seams, shown in red in A3.

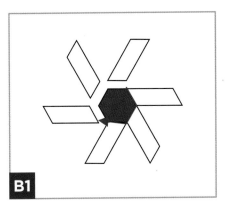

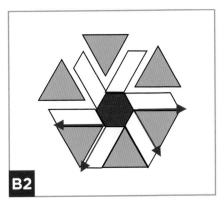

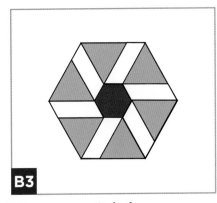

Here's another approach to similar blocks. After surrounding the center (B1), you can stitch the background pieces from their central point, outward, in two directions (B2). If you're feeling confident, however, after surrounding the center (C1), you can stitch down from one point into the concave angle, and then up the next seam, going all the way around (C2). (See Star 8 on page 77, Star 29 on page 88, and Star 92 on page 119 for the stars on this page.)

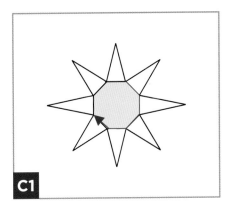

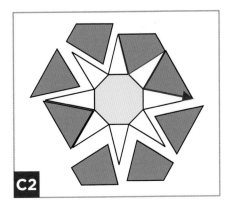

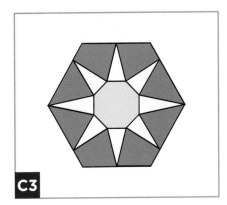

4+4 Stars

Blocks that feature shapes in multiples of four can be created by making two halves (A), and joining them along the midline (B). It can take some concentration to identify the halves. (See Star 60 on page 103 for the star below.)

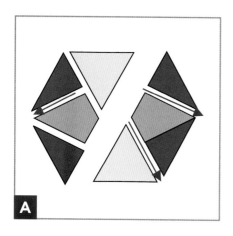 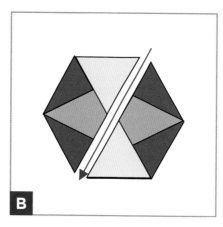 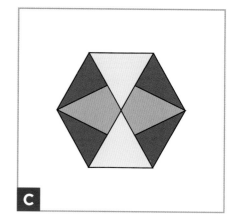

More Stars!

There are blocks that don't fit into any of the previous categories. Follow the given piecing directions, or do it your way! (For the stars below, see Star 62 on page 104, Star 85 on page 116, Star 78 on page 112, and Star 111 on page 129.)

Hand vs. Machine Piecing

HAND PIECING

This is hands-down the easiest, slowest, and most meditative method. The upside is that stitches show less than machine stitching, especially if you use thin thread (see page 9). Also, templates will come out easily, and you will probably be able to reuse them. The downside is that a complicated star can take an hour to hand stitch.

Hand piecing
(Star 10, page 78)

MACHINE PIECING

Machine piecing is much faster. Even a complicated star can be finished in less than half an hour. It's done with a tight, narrow zigzag stitch. The drawbacks with machine piecing are that the stitches will show more than if you hand stitch, and it takes experience to make adjustments in the machine. Consider the Décor Bond option (see page 14), to avoid removing templates, which can pull out stitches and/or leave bits of cardstock in the quilt if your tension and stitch size weren't perfect. (Of course, no one but you will know about the cardstock bits.)

Machine piecing
(Star 96, page 121)

Hand-Piece the Star Block Templates

BEGINNING KNOTS

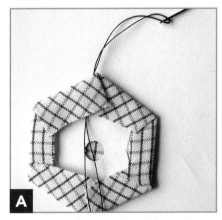

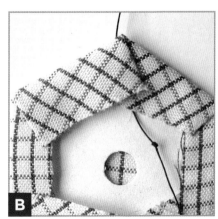

I use a single strand of thread. Any method that puts a knot near the end works. Pull the thread under (A) and into the seam allowance from the back (B). Take two more tiny stitches in place in the seam allowance to secure it.

ENDING KNOTS

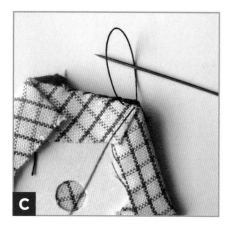 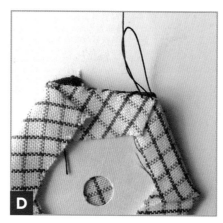 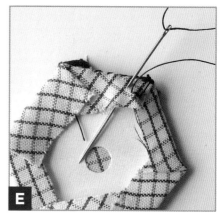

Stitch a small loop (C). Bring the needle and thread through it twice (D) and pull tight. Take two tiny stitches in place, send the needle under the seam allowance flap (E), and clip the thread.

WHIPSTITCH, RIGHT SIDES TOGETHER

I use this to join pieces with a single strand of thread. Hold the pieces, placing the good sides together, with the edges to be sewn along the top. I'm right-handed, so whenever possible, I start on the right, pinching the left ends together with my left hand (left-handers may want to do this in reverse). Pull the thread tight up to the knot and take a tiny tacking stitch.

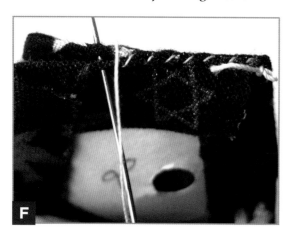

Send the needle through both fabric seam allowances, just above the templates, and then up into the air and back to the starting side. You can send the needle from back to front, or front to back (F). If corner flaps are in the way of the needle, pull or push them away so you're only catching the edge folds of each piece. At the end of each side, I like to take an extra stitch if I'm continuing to another side. When you're done, do a loop knot.

Sometimes the needle accidentally bites into the template. That's okay. You don't need to undo it, but do strive to stitch just above each template as often as possible.

WHIPSTITCH, FLAT BACK METHOD

In recent years, something known as the "flat back method," or "flat back stitch," has grown in popularity. The big advantage: stitches show significantly less from the front (compared to right sides together method). It's extremely useful for curved EPP, which is not covered in this book. If you research "flat back stitch for EPP," you will find some excellent video tutorials online.

SMOOSHING AND MUSHING, PULLING AND PUSHING

When joining edges, you can do some easing. If the corners don't match, push a bit on one side and pull on the other to align them.

When you reach the end of a seam, you often have to move the templates into a different position to stitch the next two sides. This won't harm the project. If cardstock templates pop out, either fit them back in, or remove them and sew without them.

Machine-Stitch the Star Block Templates

Machine stitching is more challenging than hand stitching. Everything happens faster, including mistakes. Practice helps A LOT. Invisible monofilament shows the least, but you could also use a decorative thread and stitch to celebrate the stitchery. See pages 9–11 for a list of the general supplies needed for machine piecing.

DO A TENSION AND TEAR TEST FIRST

Before sewing a block, do a tension, stitch, and tear test. Cut two cardstock strips, and cover each with fabric, pressing and gluing a ½" (1.3cm) seam allowance to the back. (If using Décor Bond, press it inside the fabric instead). Set the machine to a narrow zigzag (stitch length of 1.5 to 2)—as narrow as you can go without missing edges. Set a short stitch length (just shy of a satin stitch), unless you use Décor Bond, in which case the stitch can be longer. Check carefully and adjust width, length, and tension until you like the way it looks.

   Now, if you used cardstock, rip out the templates. Make sure the stitches don't rip out, too. If they do, you will need to make your stitch length even shorter (and closer to a satin stitch). Keep testing until it turns out right!

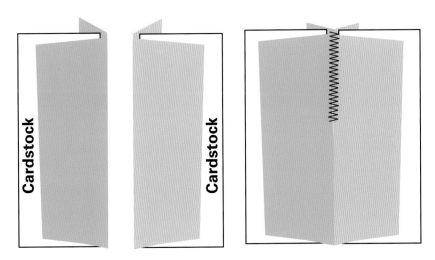

MACHINE PIECING, STEP-BY-STEP

Use the settings from your tension tests above. Here's the procedure:

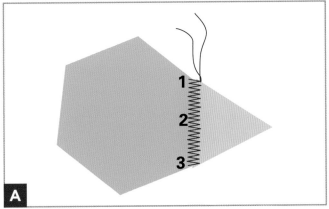

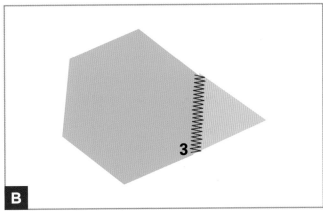

1. When possible, start with a central piece (mint-colored piece in A). Push a neighboring piece (pink) up against it with no overlap. Plant the needle in the top left corner of the central piece at position 1. Hold the threads back and steady the pieces so they don't move forward; do a couple of zigzag stitches in place.

2. Let go and sew to the end (B). Hold the pieces again to do a few more zigzags in place. If that's as far as you can go, cut the threads.

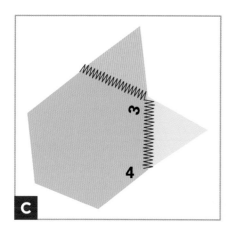

3. If you can continue adding pieces, plant the needle in the bottom left corner of the central piece at position 3 (C). Lift the presser foot and swivel the piece so the next edge lies straight in front of you. Bring up the next piece (green) and push it against the side of the central piece. Zigzag to the end at position 4 (C). If you can add more pieces to the central piece, stitch on! At some point, you'll have to cut the threads and only attach one piece at a time. Here are some more tips:

- Do a bit of easing as you sew. Keep your eyes on the ends of the templates. If they look like they're not going to match, do some gentle pushing and pulling.
- When you have a choice, stitch from wider areas toward narrow tips. Starting at the narrow tips and moving toward wider angles is less accurate, and risks the pieces going down into the needle hole, but there are times when it's impossible to avoid. If your machine has a tendency to swallow tips, you can start ¼" (0.65cm) down from the tip, back up, and then move forward.
- End each line of stitching with a couple of zigzag stitches in place, or a couple of straight back-and-forth stitches on one side.

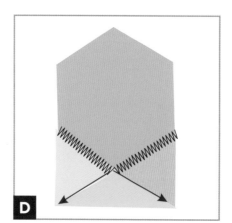
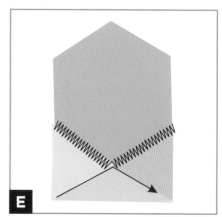

4. When you need to inset pieces, you can work from the center out (D). You can also start at one end, stitch in to the central angle, and then stitch out (E). Keep in mind that I got better at this with practice.

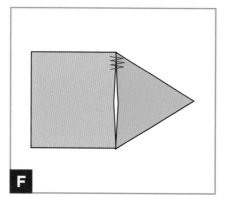
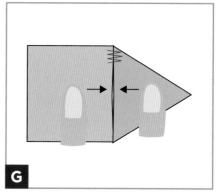

5. Sometimes there are little gaps between pieces (F). There are two ways to handle them. The first is to slide-push the fabrics together with a finger on each side to close the gap (G).

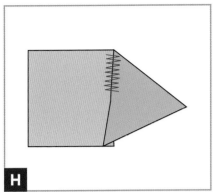

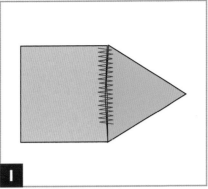

6. If the gaps are bigger, handle them like curves. Instead of "aim high" driving, aim low by focusing on what's underneath the needle. Grasp and swivel the bottom edges of each piece toward and on top of each other, as needed, take a few stitches (H), and then pull them apart again and continue stitching (I). Strive to keep the two pieces of cardstock adjacent, but don't sweat it because the worst thing that will happen is that a little cardstock overlaps and gets stuck inside. No one will suspect!

DOG-EARS BY MACHINE

A must-have tool for machine EPP is an awl, skewer, or other sharp-pointed tool. Use it to push seam-allowance flaps down and in the correct direction when machine stitching. I've found that you have to do this as you go, because you can't get them all into the proper position at the beginning of the seam. (See Star 18 on page 82 for the pattern below.)

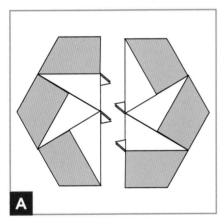

1. The block below will have four significant dog-ears (A). Tackle them one by one.

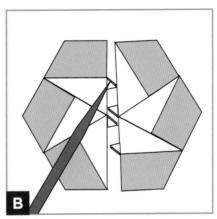

2. Push the first dog-ears under the right half (B).

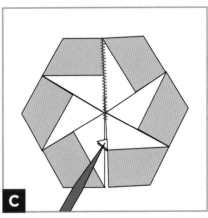

3. Stitch a little past it, stop and push the next set under the left half, and so forth to the end (C).

Save the Diagrams

After finishing a star, cut out and save the small diagrams and photos in the upper right or left corner of each pattern. Collect them in a small bag, and then conduct your own design play session, with the images of the stars you actually made, along with the small shapes. See page 138 for details.

Finishing Techniques: Piece, Appliqué, or Both

There are three ways to finish an EPP project. All can be done by **machine** or by **hand**.

1. **Piece** together the blocks and the setting shapes (the triangles, diamonds, and squares on pages 131–137), using EPP techniques on a larger scale. Leaving all templates in place, stitch each star to setting shapes and/or other stars in the same way you constructed the insides of each star block. By hand, do this with right sides together, or the flat back method, and a whipstitch (page 26). By machine, use a zigzag on top (pages 27–29). Don't remove the templates until all of the piecing is finished. Follow the principles outlined on pages 22–29. The Neutron Stars quilt on page 52 is entirely pieced. Piecing is the most labor-intensive approach, and the larger your quilt gets, the more accuracy counts.

2. **Appliqué** is a more liberating and forgiving approach. You can stitch your hexagons down pretty much anywhere you want. Remove the templates (unless you used Décor Bond), and appliqué the blocks to a background fabric. The process is similar to traditional needle-turn appliqué but easier because most edges are already turned under. The challenge is persuading some of the tails to tuck under.

3. **Combine piecing and appliqué** for maximum creative freedom. In many cases, including the Cherry Pie in the Sky (with Diamonds) quilt to the right (also, see page 56), we'll combine piecing within the multiple star formations and appliqué with all the other elements to a white background.

Facing: The Cherry Pie in the Sky (with Diamonds) quilt (see page 56) was created using piecing and appliqué techniques.

Preparing for Same-Shape Borders

If you want to appliqué, there are a couple of decisions to make. One is whether you'll appliqué by machine or by hand. Another is if you want to turn under the tails in ADVANCE of appliquéing them, or WHILE you are appliquéing them. If you want to do them in advance, you must use glue (with the same kind of glue stick as in piecing). If you choose to turn while appliquéing, no glue is needed. I've done both, and I think doing them in advance gives you a bit more control over the process.

TURNING IN ADVANCE

Say you have a formation like in the Windward project (see page 50). Let's pretend we want to appliqué it to a background. (In fact, I did a same-shape backing on this piece, which will be explained later, but the preparation is the same.)

On the bottom part, there are tails sticking out at various corners. We'll deal with them one by one. Keep the templates in place for this process.

Each tail needs to be folded backward and under. This is usually easy to do at the concave corners, but it can be a challenge at triangle tips.

Not turned yet

The easiest tails are along a flat stretch and corners that aren't sharp. Photo A shows them from the top, and photo B shows them from the back.

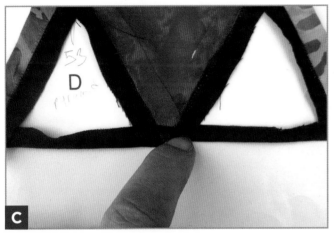

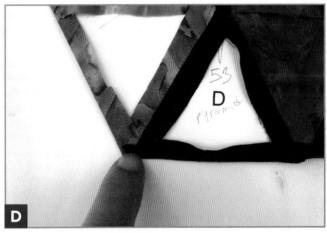

Simply fold the tails to the back and swipe with a glue stick to hold them in place (C and D). Add glue to the fabric, not to the templates (unless you used Décor Bond).

You can do a similar technique on concave angles. See the tails between the green and purple triangles in photo E? Flip the piece to the back, dab glue behind the tails, and hold them in place with a finger (F) or iron to dry the glue instantly. Make sure all of the glue is dry before pulling out the templates.

FINISHING SHARP TRIANGLE TIPS

Sharp convex angles are a challenge. I use one of two methods to get the tails out of the way in advance.

Method 1: Glue and Trim

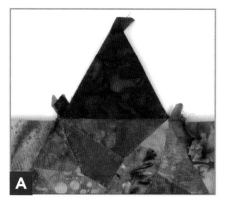

1. When you start, you'll see the triangular tips clearly.

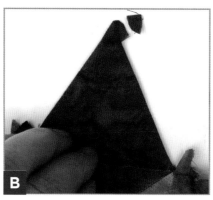

2. Trim the tail back on a diagonal.

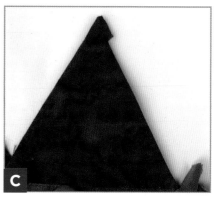

3. After trimming, the flap must still protrude a bit from top to bottom.

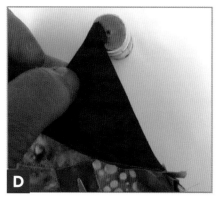

4. Dab glue on the back of the flap.

5. Fold that flap back and adjust until you can't see it from the top. This takes some fidgeting to get it right.

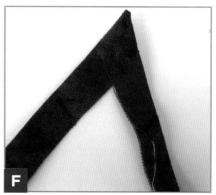

6. A view from the back when the flap is folded back on itself.

7. Here's another triangle tip folded back. Sometimes you'll need to fold it back and forth a few times to get it right.

Make sure the glue is thoroughly dry before trying to pull out the templates. If pulling them out dislodges the folds, it's easy to get them back in position. The ball-tipped stylus can help.

Method 2: Finishing Tips

This method is easier but can create tips that aren't quite as sharp. The difference is so small that it's a matter of personal preference.

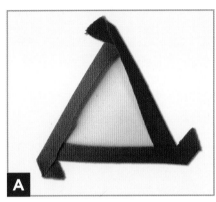

1. If you followed the directions in this book, your basted triangle looks something like this from the back. You will probably only need to clean up one tip this way—one that isn't attached to another piece.

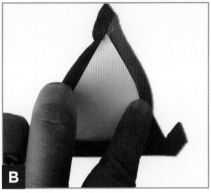

2. Open up the tip you want to finish. If you glue-basted it, you might need to spritz a few drops of water to loosen the glue. Press it flat.

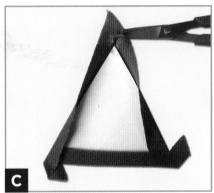

3. Trim off the tip. There should still be a scant ¼" (0.65cm) of fabric above the template tip.

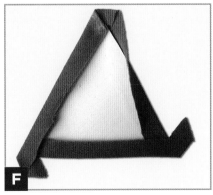

5. Fold in one side, pressing the fold close against the template by hand or with an iron.

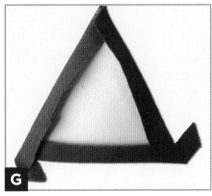

6. Fold in the other side. Note: in this case, it doesn't matter which side you fold in first.

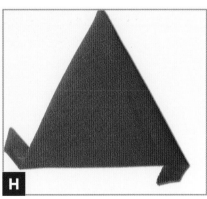

4. Apply a dab of glue to the tip and fold it straight down. Press if possible.

7. Here's your triangle with a finished tip, ready to be appliquéd to a background or stitched to a backing.

The Appliqué Process

Double-check that you've removed all of the templates. Don't worry about any bits left in the seams.

Tape the background fabric to a tabletop or a floor, just taut enough so that it's wrinkle free. Pin the top, whether it's one block or a formation, to the background fabric. If it's a large project, you may now want to thread-baste it so you don't poke yourself with pins during machine or hand appliqué.

Important: If you didn't prepare the piece for appliqué in advance, don't push the tails under at this basting stage. Instead, you will push them under as you do the permanent stitching. Also, whether you sew by hand or machine, the following rule is important: If your seam allowances and tails stick out **clockwise** (from the top)—as shown in the second diagram—sew **clockwise** around the blocks and formations. If the seam allowances and tails point **counterclockwise** from the front, sew **counterclockwise** (more on that later).

APPLIQUÉ BY HAND

Use the same needles and threads I recommended for hand piecing (on page 9) or use your favorites. Push each tail or seam allowance under as you get to them if you didn't treat them already. (See page 46 for the project below.)

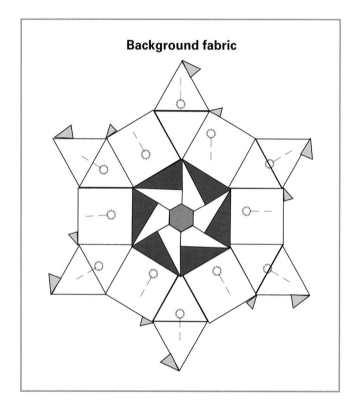

Background fabric

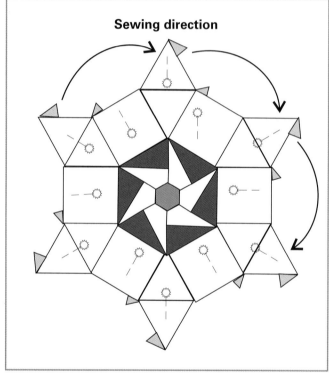

Sewing direction

APPLIQUÉ BY MACHINE

My favorite thread for this process is invisible monofilament thread. My machine does well with it on top and in the bobbin, but you can use whatever thread you like. (If you choose invisible for the bobbin, don't load the bobbin more than half-full; the stretchiness can break the bobbin.)

- Keep handy a small, sharp pair of scissors, small pins, and an awl.
- Set a zigzag, blanket, or other wide stitch to a comfortable stitch width of about 3, and of medium-short length. Unlike machine piecing EPP, the appliqué stitch doesn't have to be close to a satin stitch. It can be as tight or loose as you like.
- Test the tension first by making up a similar sample.

1. If you didn't turn under the tips in advance, now's a good time to cut back extra-long tails. Leave a little sticking out to bend under.

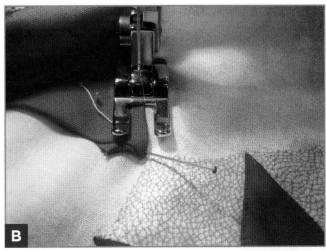

2. Do the zigzag, blanket, or another wide stitch on straight paths all the way to the tip, which should be pointing in the opposite direction.

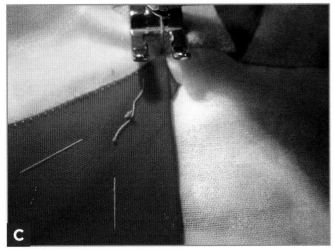

3. Plant the needle just above the tip on the background fabric and turn the fabric. Use your awl or a pin to tuck the seam allowance under.

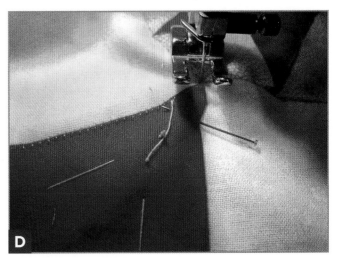

4. Sometimes you may need a small pin to hold the tail under.

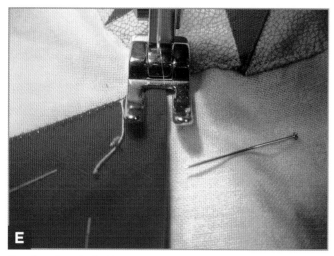

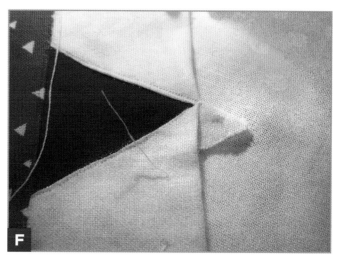

5. Slowly stitch down, removing any pin just before you get to it.

6. Sometimes, you have to push the tail in the opposite direction of the way it's naturally folded. For example, in the photo above, the machine is in the middle of a star block side, approaching a tail.

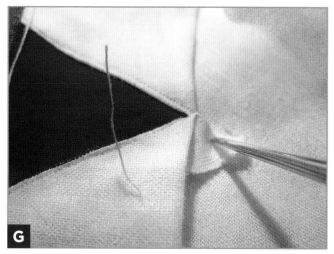

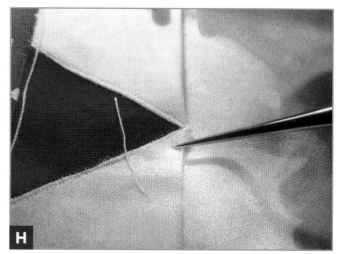

7. When it gets close, use the awl to push the tail backward and under (G). Pushing it forward doesn't work! Use the awl (or a pin) to hold it down until the last second and then remove the pin and stitch past that point (H).

8. Once everything is appliquéd, you may opt to cut away the fabric behind the formations. I usually do that only for large formations, not single blocks. Cutting makes quilting easier and potentially neater, so you won't wind up scooting the appliqués into wrinkles. On the other hand, leaving the backing in place makes the quilt stronger, especially if it's going to receive heavy use as a bed quilt.

Removing Templates

As useful as the templates are in the beginning of your quilt journey, there comes a time for you to remove them. The process is slightly different for hand- and machine-stitched pieces.

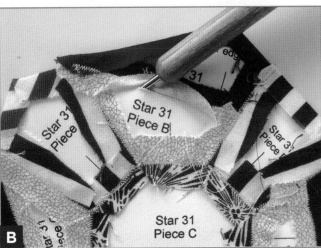

1. Start by gently pulling on the block, lengthwise and widthwise. You may hear and feel some of the templates breaking free from the seams.

2. Slide the large end of a ball-tip stylus under the glued seam allowances, all the way around (A). If you machine-stitched, rub the ball tip against the stitching.

3. Slide the tool underneath a cardstock edge and pry upward. Repeat on as many sides as needed (B).

4. With your fingers, pull the template in the direct opposite direction from any small points.

5. Examine the piece you pulled out. Are there large pieces missing? If so, a hemostat or tweezers will help you get deep inside to pull out the rest.

6. If you machine-pieced your project, no matter how diligent you are, there will be bits of cardstock left inside. Don't worry; no one will know!

Finishing Quilt Edges, Straight or Odd Shapes

If you're in a hurry, you dislike handwork, or you have an oddly shaped piece, it's easiest to appliqué it to a fabric square or rectangle, and then finish the edges with a traditional quilt binding.

One of the charms of EPP quilts, however, is that the edges have surprising angles. If you want to preserve them, you can stitch the top to a same-shape backing. The process is similar to needle-turn appliqué, except you're turning under two raw edges at the same time on the top and the backing fabrics. Tips and concave angles can be especially challenging. Here's how I do it:

1. Place the top on a larger piece of batting. Lay those on an even larger backing fabric, right side down (A). Pin around the edges of the top, about 1" (2.55cm) in from the edges.

2. With sharp, small scissors, cut the batting about ⅛" (0.3cm) smaller than the top. (In photo B, the batting is half-trimmed.) Don't cut into the backing yet!

3. Trim the backing fabric about ½" (1.3cm) bigger than the top (C).

4. Clip straight into the backing at all concave angles (red arrows in D). Clip to just beyond the edge of the batting. Option: you can pin both edges inward in advance or do it as you sew.

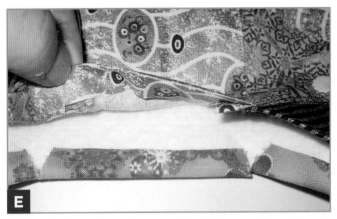

5. Load a hand-sewing needle with matching thread. Bit by bit, fold the backing's raw edges inward, over the batting, and then whipstitch the top and bottom folds together (E).

6. At clipped angles, fold the seam allowances in as far as they go, so that a couple of threads are turned inside (F). Use your needle tip to sweep the clipped corner within the folds.

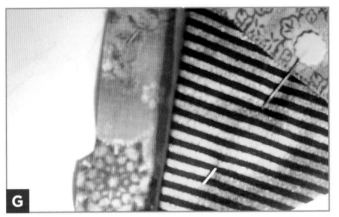

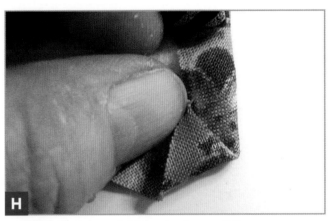

7. At triangle points, fold the backing's seam allowance over (G) and then fold its tip down (H).

8. Push the remaining raw edge inward (I). Stitch it to the tip of the top's backing (J), tucking the top's tail inside. I know this seems complicated at first, but I promise it will get easier with practice.

FAQ about Hexagon Stars

Before you begin making your stars, here are some important answers on how to read and work with the patterns.

WHAT DO THE MARKINGS MEAN?

The arrows point to the center of each hexagon. The center is also marked with a dot when necessary. I put arrows only on pieces that can become confusing when they've been cut out.

The letters signify which piece it is. In the half-pattern on the right, you can see pieces A, B, and C. Pieces with the same letter are the same shape and size.

DO I WORK FROM THE FRONT OR BACK?

The full-size pattern for each star shows the back of the block. Baste the cardstock pieces to the WRONG SIDE of the fabric with all of the markings facing UP at you so you can read them throughout the piecing process.

Next to each pattern, there's a diagram and a photo that show the finished FRONT of the block (so it's a mirror image of the larger cutting pattern). **Refer to these images while constructing the block.**

When you're done making the block, cut out and save these diagrams to help you play with design (see page 140).

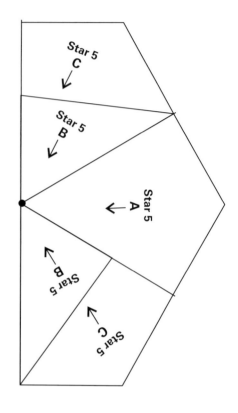

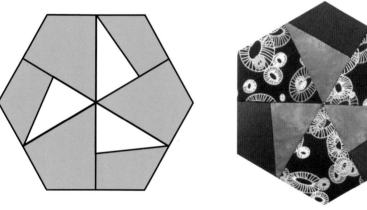

Star 5 Front   **On point**

Star 19

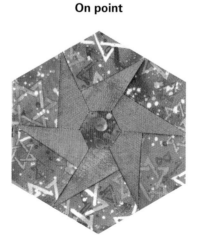

Star 21

WHY DO SOME STARS HAVE A CENTERPIECE?

I want to give you creative choices! Notice the difference between Stars 19 and 21. Star 19 doesn't have a centerpiece; Star 21 has a hexagon in the middle. You can also appliqué a different centerpiece any time you want (or maybe a button!).

Star 17   **Star 18**

WHY ARE THERE MIRROR IMAGES OF SOME BLOCKS?

On the left are Stars 17 and 18, which are mirror images of one another. One of my goals is to create quilts with motion. Stars that spin in different directions help achieve that.

WHY WATCH THE CORNERS?

With my first EPP project (the grouping below left), I learned that if all the blocks have corner seams, joining them neatly will be challenging. The second photo shows one of that project's intersections: a meeting of nine seams! It was a hot mess, and I had to take it out and do it all over more carefully. The blocks eventually became part of my Neutron Star quilt project (page 52).

My first EPP project

Nine seams met in this intersection, which made things messy.

For this reason, about half the blocks in this book don't have corner seams or only have a few. Things will go more smoothly if you alternate adjoining stars that that do and don't have corner seams, *whenever possible*.

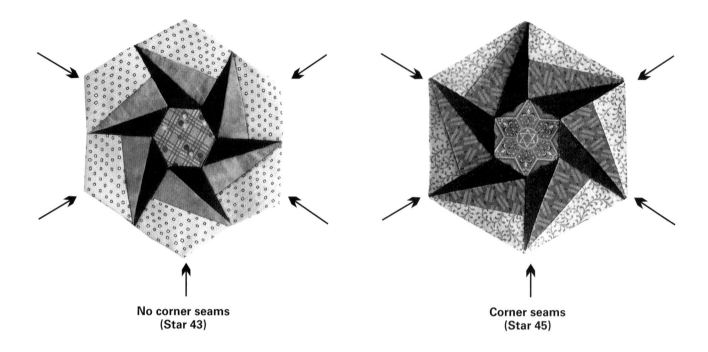

No corner seams
(Star 43)

Corner seams
(Star 45)

Similarly, if your blocks join along straight edges, avoid connecting blocks with seams in the same place. This is not an absolute rule, but things come together more easily when seams don't bump into each other.

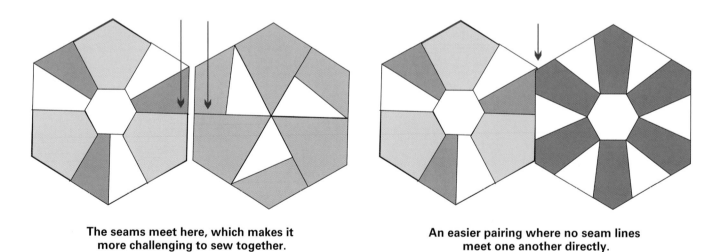

The seams meet here, which makes it
more challenging to sew together.

An easier pairing where no seam lines
meet one another directly.

PROJECTS

Throughout this project section, you will find some really fun projects to practice your EPP skills. They range in difficulty, from easy to advanced. You may use the same star blocks as I did, but I also encourage you to choose your own. For all star block patterns, please see pages 74–130.

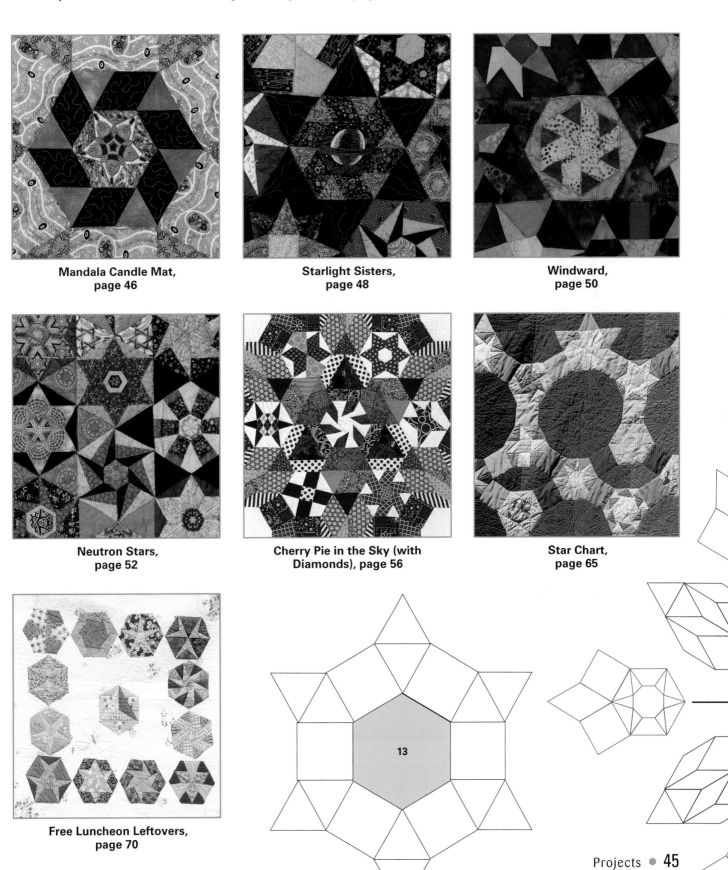

**Mandala Candle Mat,
page 46**

**Starlight Sisters,
page 48**

**Windward,
page 50**

**Neutron Stars,
page 52**

**Cherry Pie in the Sky (with
Diamonds), page 56**

**Star Chart,
page 65**

**Free Luncheon Leftovers,
page 70**

Mandala Candle Mat

This project requires very little fabric, making it an ideal scrap project! You only need to make one star block; I used Star 13, but you can use whichever one you like. For the central hexagon, I fussy-cut a printed star, and I fussy-cut the stripes in the outer triangles, so they're all angled the same way.

1. Photocopy and print one copy of the setting triangle template (see pages 133 or 134), and one copy of the setting square (see page 136), onto cardstock or Décor bond. (If you prefer, you can rotary-cut the square templates.) If your printer doesn't cooperate with cardstock or Décor Bond, you can photocopy the pages and glue them to cardstock. More printout advice and information is on page 12.

2. Cut the shapes from your photocopies or printouts. Use those paper shapes to cut six oversized fabric triangles from the darkest fabric, and six more triangles from the medium fabric. Cut the squares from the lightest fabric.

1 star block
Setting shapes
• 12 equilateral triangles
• 6 squares
Finished size: 16" x 16" (40.65 x 40.65cm)

Fabric
• Enough for 1 star block
• 1 fat quarter each of a light, medium, and dark color for the setting shapes

Star Pattern:
• Star 13: page 80

3. Baste the fabric to each setting shape template, following the steps on pages 17–21.

4. Following the diagram on this page, stitch a basted square to each side of the central block's six edges. In each corner, insert six equilateral triangles.

5. Add the six outward-pointing triangles in the second color. Remove all of the templates (see page 39).

6. Here are your finishing options:

- Appliqué the formation to a square or rectangular piece of fabric. In that case, it can easily be finished with a standard quilt binding.
- If you want to preserve the uneven edge, follow the directions on pages 40–41, which is what I did with this quilt. You'll be stitching the front to a same-shape backing.

7. As you can see in the photo, I did some free-motion stippling in the center block and wavy lines tracking the print in the squares. I quilted next to the seam lines inside the medium equilateral triangles to define the shapes.

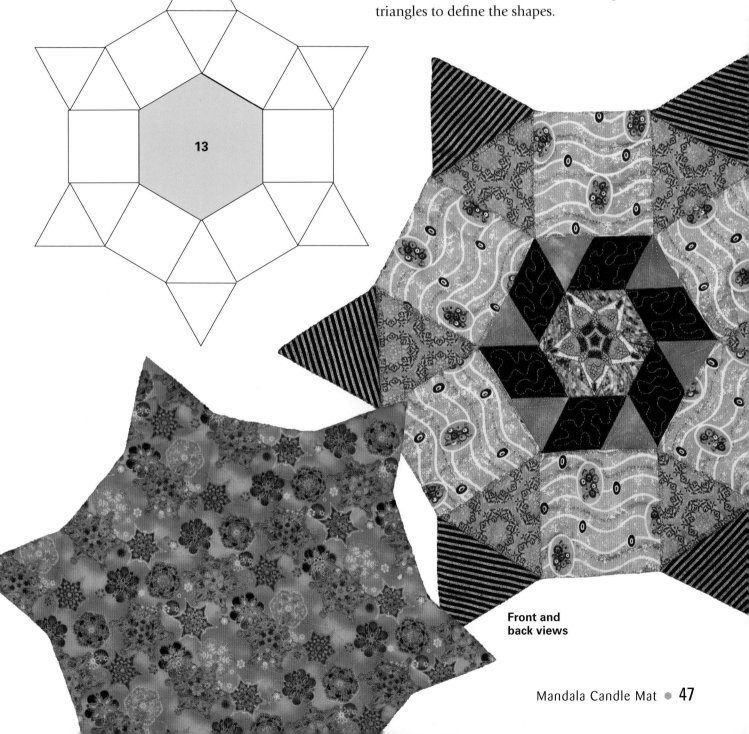

13

Front and back views

Mandala Candle Mat • **47**

Starlight Sisters

This table topper or wall hanging has seven star blocks in a traditional Seven Sisters arrangement. Protruding squares make it unique. When used on a table, the squares serve as built-in coasters.

Along with star block fabrics in assorted blue and gold prints, you'll need a ¼ yard (0.25m), or fat-quarter, of one fabric for the setting triangles (a solid navy blue here), and another ¼ yard (0.25m), or fat quarter, for the squares (a striped print in mine.)

1. Make seven star blocks. Choose the ones I did (listed in the sidebar) or pick your own, keeping the following in mind:

- Alternate blocks with corner seams, touching those without corner seams. Reducing corner seams helps blocks come together neatly. (Read more about why this is important on page 43.) Unfortunately for me, I used Star 14 in the center; its corner seams made piecing more challenging than it needed to be. That's why I strongly suggest you choose a different block, one without corner seams, for your central position.
- Mix up "spin" direction to give the piece motion.

7 star blocks
Setting shapes
- 12 equilateral triangles
- 12 squares
Finished size:
25" (63.5cm) across at its widest

Fabric
- Small amounts for 7 star blocks, plus 1 dark fat quarter or ¼ yard (0.25m) for the 12 setting triangles
- Fat quarter, or ¼ yard (0.25m), for the 12 squares

Star Pattern:
- Star 8: page 77
- Star 14: page 80
- Star 22: page 84
- Star 25: page 86
- Star 44: page 95
- Star 59: page 103
- Star 71: page 109

2. This design has twelve setting equilateral triangles and twelve squares. Print out one copy of the triangles (see pages 133 or 134) onto cardstock, paper, or Décor Bond. Print out two copies of the setting square templates (see page 136) or rotary-cut the square templates. Follow the directions starting on page 12 to print out the templates, cut the fabric, and baste the setting shapes to the fabric.

3. Following the diagram below, stitch six setting triangles around the central star block. Inset the six remaining star blocks, and then inset the outer ring of triangles. Finally, add the squares.

4. Remove the cardstock templates.

5. Follow the directions on pages 40–41 to add backing. Trim, turn edges inward, push tails inward, and finish edges with hand stitching.

6. Quilt as desired. I used gold metallic thread. First, I stitched "in the ditch" (next to the ditch) for the largest shapes within each star block. I then added emanating wavy lines over the setting triangles. Even though I left my squares unquilted, you could choose to quilt circles or hexagons in those spaces if you wish.

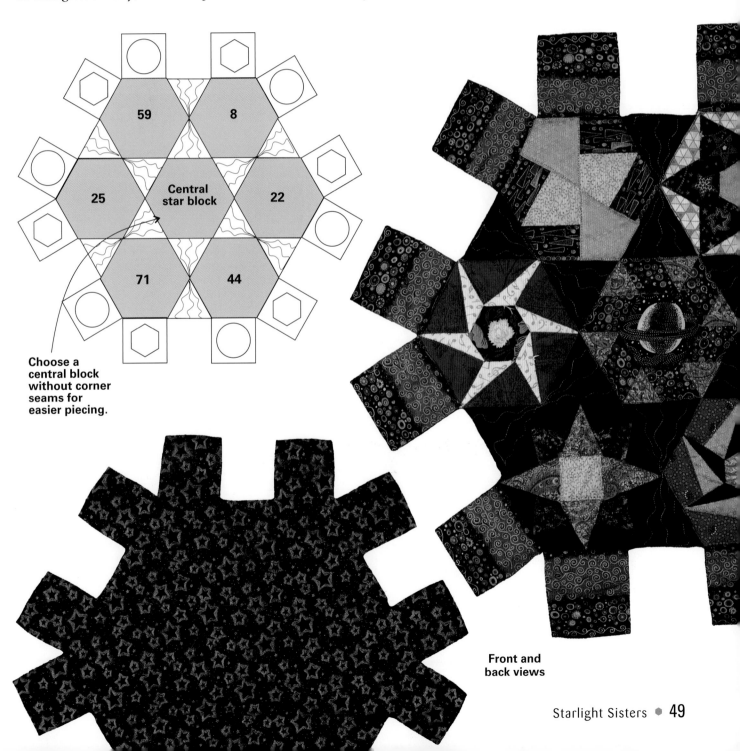

59

8

25

Central star block

22

71

44

Choose a central block without corner seams for easier piecing.

Front and back views

Windward

This table runner is ideal for using up scraps and/or precuts. I made it with batiks, but it would also look good in solids. When I was finished, I thought it looked like a bunch of windmills, so that's why I called it "Windward."

1. This design requires forty-four equilateral setting triangles and ten regular setting diamonds. Copy and print four copies of page 133 onto cardstock, paper, or Décor Bond to make all of these shapes.

2. Make eleven star blocks. For the seven that touch in the central "seven sisters" formation (blocks in positions 1 to 7 in the colorful diagram on the next page), make four without corner seams and the remaining three with corner seams. Alternate them around the circle. The central block should not have corner seams. (The four outer blocks in positions 8 to 10 in the diagram on the next page don't touch each other, so you can choose any seam configuration.)

11 star blocks
Setting shapes
- 44 equilateral triangles
- 10 regular diamonds
Finished size: 21" x 33"
(53.35 x 83.8cm)

Fabric
- Various batik scraps and/ or precuts

Star Pattern:
- Star 12: page 79
- Star 40: page 93
- Star 56: page 101
- Star 97: page 122
- Star 98: page 122
- Star 101: page 124
- Star 102: page 124
- Star 104: page 125
- Star 105: page 126
- Star 107: page 127
- Star 108: page 127

3. Use the diagrams below to plan color placement. I repeated fabrics for some of the setting shapes. For example, I used a streaky magenta/purple batik fabric for the six equilateral triangles A to F that surround the central star. I used a medium blue fabric for the six equilateral triangles in positions G through L that surround stars 1 to 7.

4. Triangles N and M, on the outer sides of the block in positions 7 and 4, are the same pinkish/orange fabric. The two triangles P on the far sides of the formation are purple, and the two O triangles touching the P triangles are red.

5. Six of the diamonds Z2, V, and U on both sides of the formation are a streaky green. The four diamonds T and Z1 (also on both sides of the formation) are a purple-colored batik. The equilateral triangles in positions aa, bb, cc, dd, and ee along the top and bottom of the central formation bb and dd are a dark navy blue fabric. The triangles aa, cc, and ee are made from various colors. The ff triangles are a very light blue.

6. I constructed each arm separately. On the left wing, I surrounded stars in positions 8 and 9 separately with their setting shapes. I did the same on the right side for stars 10 and 11. Then I joined formation 8 to 9 and formation 10 to 11. Finally, I joined the left and right arms to the center.

7. The easiest finishing method is to appliqué the piece to a rectangle of fabric. To make it more challenging, cut a same-shape batting and backing, and appliqué the top to the bottom. See page 36 for directions.

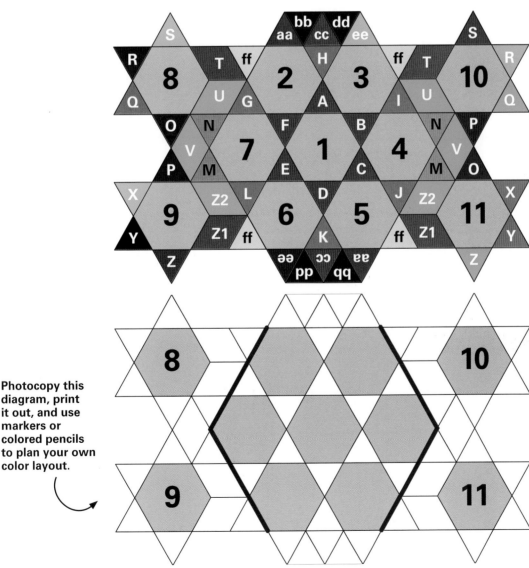

Photocopy this diagram, print it out, and use markers or colored pencils to plan your own color layout.

Neutron Stars

This quilt hangs in my husband's office. He's an astrophysicist and studies neutron stars, which, he has explained to me, are the heaviest stars with the highest density. They occasionally crash together in massive explosions, creating heavy elements like gold and plutonium. Therefore, I named this dense hand-pieced quilt "Neutron Stars."

Setting Shapes

Because this quilt is so complex, I decided to simplify the instructions by using abbreviations in the step-by-step text and diagrams.

- **T** = Equilateral triangles. Baste seventy-two.
- **BT** = Top and bottom border triangle. These are the same size and shape as the equilateral triangles, but you may want to use different fabrics. Baste twelve.
- **SD** = Split diamond for top and bottom borders. Baste twenty.
- **HETR** = Half-equilateral triangle right-hand piece, for the edges of the borders. Make four.
- **HETL** = Half-equilateral triangle left-hand piece, for the edges of the borders. Make four.

16 star blocks
Setting shapes
- 72 equilateral triangles
- 12 top and bottom border triangles
- 20 split diamonds
- 4 right half-equilateral triangles
- 4 left half-equilateral triangles

Finished size: 30" x 42" (76.2 x 106.7cm)

Fabrics
- Small amounts of 20+ prints and solids in blues, whites, and golds

Star Patterns:
- Star 7: page 77
- Star 8: page 77
- Star 9: page 78
- Star 19: page 83
- Star 20: page 83
- Star 21: page 84
- Star 26: page 86
- Star 27: page 87
- Star 29: page 88
- Star 30: page 88
- Star 32: page 89
- Star 37: page 92
- Star 43: page 95
- Star 45: page 96

1. This layout requires thirty-six stars. They will be placed in six vertical columns, each six blocks high. When I started, I had only designed Star 8, so you'll notice it repeated a couple of times in the diagram on page 54. As I worked on this book, I designed new stars and added a few in. A more diverse and much easier layout is suggested in the diagram on page 55. For energy and motion, neighboring stars in the diagram reverse direction, and I tried to place the blocks with corner seams so they touched those without as often as possible.

2. Prepare your background shapes. Baste seventy-two equilateral setting triangles (T), twelve top and bottom border triangles (BT), and twenty split diamonds (SD). For the border edge pieces, make four right-hand and four left-hand half-equilateral triangles (HETR and HETL, respectively).

3. In the first column, sew two T pieces above the top star block (Star 8). Then sew two more T pieces below the block. Add a second star block, and then two T pieces under that. Follow that by adding the next star block, and then two T pieces, continuing in this fashion until you reach the end of the column.

4. When each column is complete, add the BT units (which are also equilateral triangles) to the top or bottom of the columns that require them.

5. Join the columns along the vertical seams. Lastly, add the SD units and the half-equilateral triangles in the four outer corners (templates on page 132). Remove the cardstock templates.

6. Add the batting and backing and finish as described on page 40, cutting the batting slightly smaller than the top and the backing a bit bigger. Clip the concave curves on the back and whipstitch the folded edges closed. You could also baste the whole thing to a larger background piece for instant borders. In that case, you can finish with a traditional quilt binding.

Neutron Stars, as in the photo

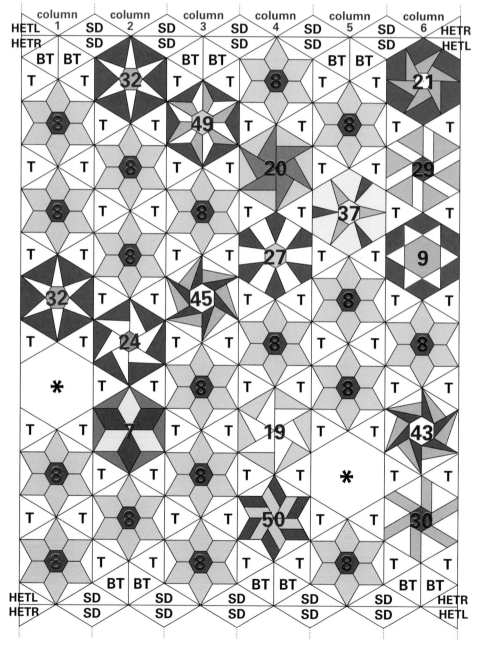

* For technical reasons, blocks with an asterisk were not included in this book. Please feel free to fill it in with any star block you wish. You may also use the variation diagram on the next page.

I used *Star Trek* fabric for the back and hanging sleeve of this quilt.

Neutron Stars, easier and improved layout

Variation Diagram

Cherry Pie in the Sky (with Diamonds)

This large quilt combines appliqué with piecing. I did the appliqué by machine with invisible monofilament thread, but you can also do it by hand and/or use any thread you like. The setting shapes listed at the top of this page are those I used in the central formation only. If you wish, you may choose to add more to the arm extensions.

42 star blocks

Setting shapes (in central formation)
- 12 squares
- 18 equilateral triangles
- 18 regular diamonds
- 24 narrow diamonds
- 6 spacer hexagons (see page 64)

Finished size: 62" x 82"
(157.5 x 208.3cm)

Fabrics
- 3 yards (2.75m) of an ultra wide white fabric (about 90"+ [228.6cm+]) or 7 yards (6.4m) of a regular width white fabric if you don't mind a seam in the front
- Assorted scraps of red solids, white solids, and red-and-white prints

Star Patterns:
- Star 7: page 77
- Star 8: page 77
- Star 15: page 81
- Star 26: page 86
- Star 27: page 87
- *Star 40: page 93
- Star 44: page 95
- Star 47: page 97
- Star 52: page 99
- Star 54: page 100
- Star 55: page 101
- Star 56: page 101

- Star 57: page 102
- Star 61: page 104
- Star 62: page 104
- Star 63: page 105
- Star 64: page 105
- Star 67: page 107
- Star 68: page 107
- Star 69: page 108
- Star 72: page 109
- Star 73: page 110
- Star 74: page 110
- Star 77: page 112
- Star 78: page 112

- Star 79: page 113
- Star 80: page 113
- Star 84: page 115
- Star 85: page 116
- Star 86: page 116
- Star 89: page 118
- Star 90: page 118
- Star 91: page 119
- Star 93: page 120
- Star 94: page 120
- Star 97: page 122
- Star 98: page 122
- Star 100: page 123

* I have added an additional appliqué element to the center of Star 40.

Note: A double asterisk in the diagram means that the star block pattern was not included in this book for technical reasons. Please substitute another star block in these instances, keeping in mind corner or side seams.

1. Construct the large formation diagrammed below. It contains seven stars; the block numbers I used are in red print, but you can pick your own. Mix up the spin directions in the blocks to give the quilt motion.

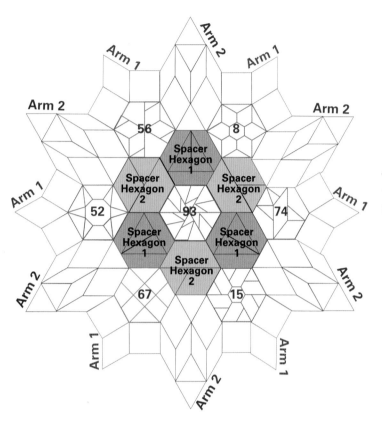

2. Make six "spacer hexagons," shown as gray in the diagram. Mine are shown below. The patterns for these easy blocks are on page 64. There are two types for this project, Spacer Hexagons 1 and 2.

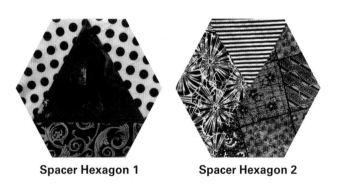

Spacer Hexagon 1   Spacer Hexagon 2

3. Assemble and make six Arm 2 units. The central formation has two different arms, each repeated six times. The setting shapes listed on page 56 shows how many you'll need to print out and baste.

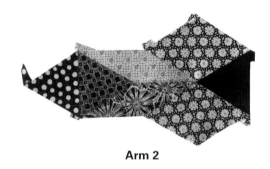

Arm 2

4. Create the spacer hexagons and attach each Arm 2 to a spacer hexagon. Below is an Arm 2 attached to a Spacer Hexagon 2.

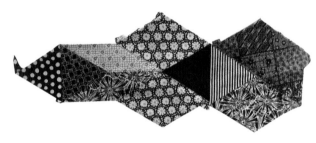

Arm 2 with Spacer Hexagon 2

5. I started in the center, surrounding Star 93 with the six spacer hexagons that were already attached to their Arm 2 units.

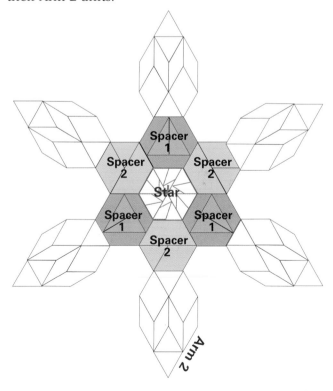

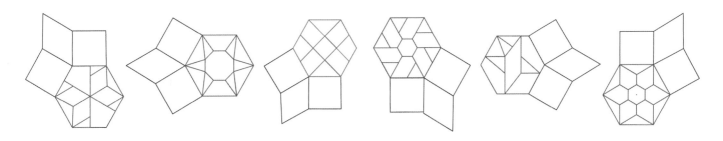

6. Stitch two squares and then a diamond (the components of Arm 1) to the outer two edges of the star blocks (or do this after step 8).

7. Inset these stars attached to Arm 1 in the spaces in between the Arm 2 units.

8. Sew up any remaining seams, and you've completed the first phase! Full disclosure: when I got to this step, my central star block took on a slightly volcanic shape. Thankfully, I was able to quilt it out. At this point, I like to celebrate my new formation by taking lots of pictures of it, posing with family members and well-known buildings.

Arm 1

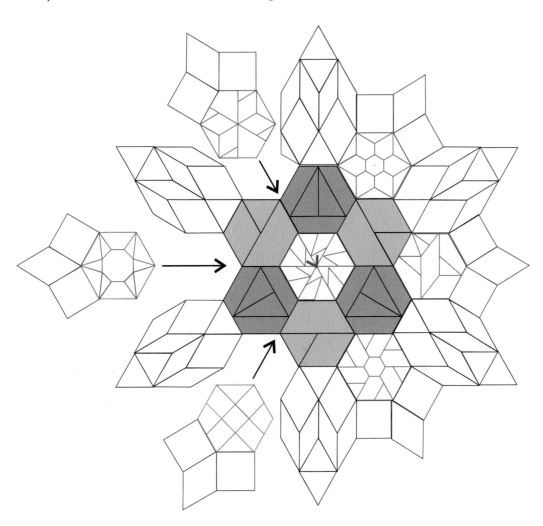

Take lots of photos of your work-in-progress.

**I always find that the back can be just
as interesting as the front.**

Above are pictures I took of my daughter holding it on our (nonfamous) front porch. The back is as interesting as the front!

9. When you're finished taking pictures, pull out the templates. Find a comfortable seat, bring over a trash can, put on your magnifying glasses, and wield your ball-tipped stylus. If you hand-sewed the star together, you can probably reuse most of the templates. (If you machine-stitched, you'll probably end up filling the trashcan.) If you used Décor Bond, skip this step entirely!

10. You can take a "break" at this point . . . by making more star blocks! If you're replicating my layout, you need to make thirty-five more stars. Please note that some of the blocks I used in this quilt are not located in Part IV of this book. Due to technical reasons, I had to leave them out (indicated with a double asterisk on the diagram). You may substitute these blocks with any others you find on pages 74–130.

11. Let's call the blocks and formations that are beyond the main formation "arm extensions." There are twelve arm extensions. Some of them are lone

blocks, but six of them—from the 5 o'clock to the 10 o'clock positions in the diagram on the next page—contain small formations, like the one in the photo below (it's at 7 o'clock on the quilt). See the white triangles within it? They are not windows. I decided it would be easier to piece in a white triangle of fabric, basted to an equilateral triangle template, like all the other setting shapes.

The white triangles in the left image are pieced as a part of the arm extension, rather than windows that allow the background fabric show through. The image on the right is an example of an arm extension.

12. Sew together your formations. Follow my structures (in the diagram, star blocks are gray) or make up your own. The solo star blocks that just touch each other (from 11 o'clock to 1 o'clock and parts of some other arm extensions) will be appliquéd to the background one by one.

13. Remove all papers from the blocks and formations.

14. Prepare the background: inspect it to make sure it's clean and pressed, and launder it if necessary. If you bought 3 yards (2.75m) of an ultrawide fabric (anything wider than 63" [160cm]), cut it to 63" x 83" (160 x 210.85cm). If you're starting with 6 yards (5.5m) of a regular-width fabric, cut it into two 3-yard (2.75-m) pieces and stitch them

together. Trim about 9" (22.85cm) off one vertical edge to make the entire width 63" (160cm). Lay the background fabric on a flat surface. I find it helpful to lightly tape it in place, but don't pull it taut.

15. Pin the blocks and formations to the background fabric. After placing and pinning the large formation, I pinned one extension arm at a time, using a yardstick (meter stick) to make sure all of the pieces were in a straight line, extending from the dead center of the large formation's central block and running through the center of each extension piece and block. After pin-basting, thread-baste everything down to eliminate the chance of stabbing yourself with pins during the appliqué process. In the photo below, you can see the large stitches of the thread basting.

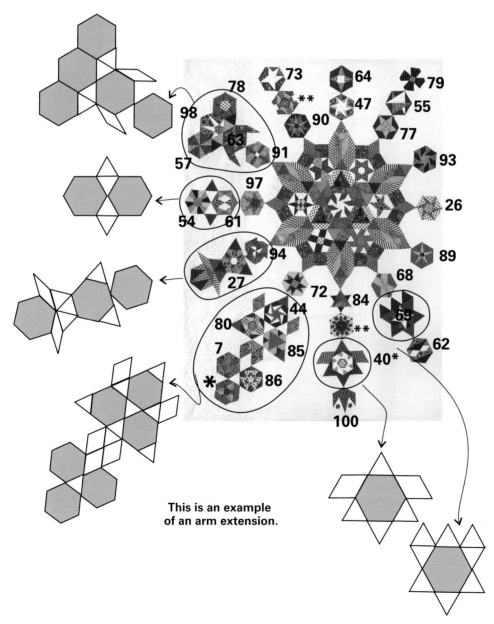

This is an example of an arm extension.

16. Appliqué of EPPed stars, setting shapes, and combinations are very similar to traditional needle-turn appliqué. It's a little easier because the edges are already turned under. The greatest challenge is persuading the tails to tuck neatly underneath. Pages 36–38 in this book explain how to appliqué by hand or machine.

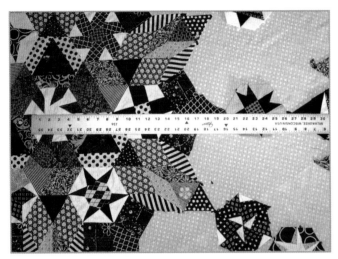

Make sure all the arm extensions lay in a straight line.

Your thread-basting stitches don't have to be pretty, just secure.

17. What about quilting? Even with all those stars, there's a lot of white space. I took a divide-and-conquer approach. The sketch here gives you the main idea. The green lines denote where I did a double-sided vine/feathers, circling around the main formation. The emanating dark purple lines show where I stitched double lines, about ¼" (0.65cm) apart. This created subdivisions. Each subdivision contains a different free-motion quilting design. I also surrounded each appliqué with quilting. The outlined hexagon stars show where I quilted star designs turned into quilting motifs. If you're interested in trying this, see the next page.

I did some free-motion quilting in all the white spaces.

Turning Straight-Line Piecing Patterns into Curvy Quilting Motifs

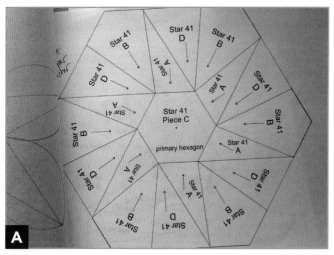

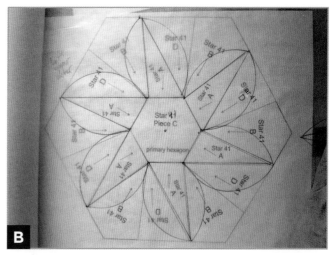

1. Print out the star you want to use as a quilting motif. I printed Star 41 on regular paper (A). Then I laid tracing paper (Golden Threads Quilting Paper) on top of the block and drew curves to substitute for straight lines (B). DO NOT USE A PENCIL for this tracing. Otherwise, when you stitch through it, you may get pencil marks on your quilt. Instead, use a fine-point permanent or washable marker.

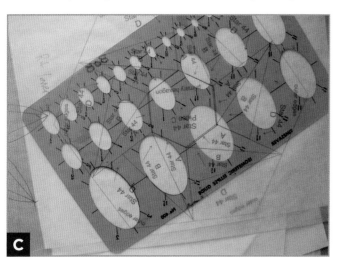

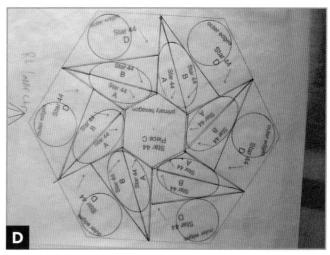

2. I either drew the curves freehand or used nearby jars, circle stencils, or oval stencils (C). I found a circular and oval stencil to be useful for Star 44 (D).

3. Give your tracing lines a few minutes to dry before stitching through them. Once dry, pin the stencil to the quilt (photo E) and stitch through it. I like Golden Threads paper because it shatters easily and doesn't pull stitches out with it when you rip it away, unlike regular copy paper. If you want to try a different tracing paper, do a test first to make sure it rips out cleanly before doing it on your finished quilt.

4. Finish with a binding and enjoy your new quilt!

Spacer Hexagon 1

Print three copies of this page to make the three blocks that surround the central star in the Cherry Pie quilt.

Spacer Hexagon 1
C →

← Spacer Hexagon 1
C

Spacer
Hexagon 1
B

Spacer
Hexagon 1
A

↑
C
Spacer Hexagon 1

Front

C A B C
C

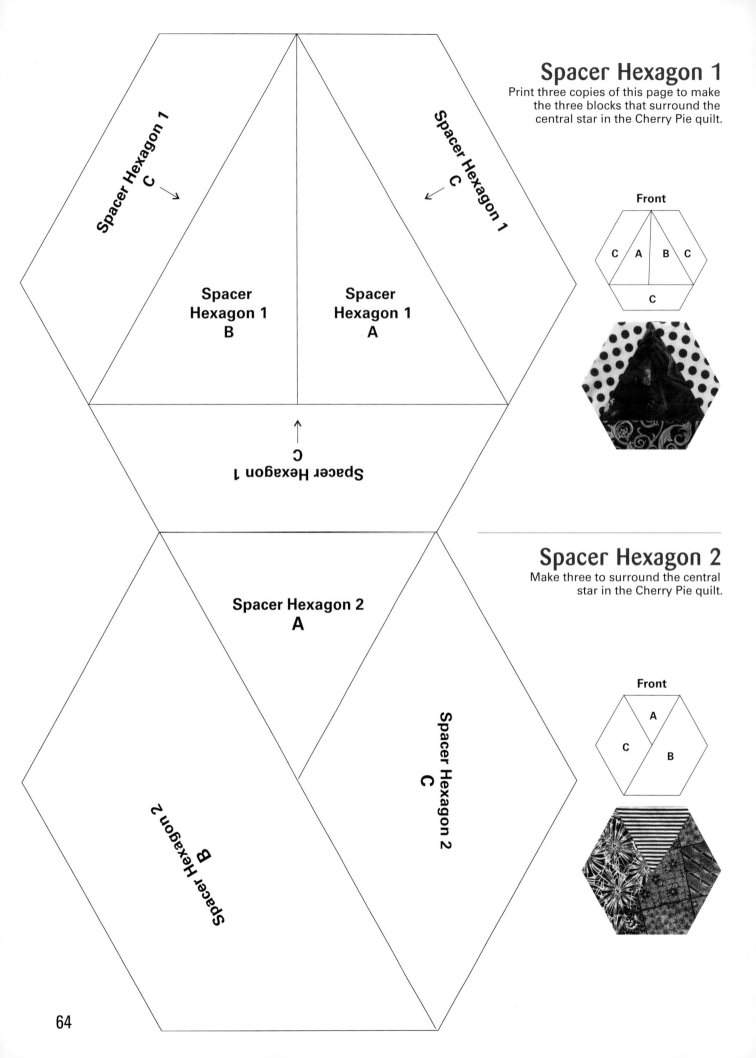

Spacer Hexagon 2

Make three to surround the central star in the Cherry Pie quilt.

Spacer Hexagon 2
A

Spacer Hexagon 2
C

Spacer Hexagon 2
B

Front

A
C
B

Star Chart

As I developed this quilt, I found myself thinking about mass transit posters, and I imagined the trails of color as train routes: the Green Line, the Blue Line, the Red Line . . . these maps are works of art designed by very talented people. This is especially true in the complicated cities I've been lucky enough to live in, including Boston, Tokyo, and now Los Angeles (where I can walk to the real-life Gold Line!). With this in mind, it's not surprising that, instead of a quilt about stars, I wound up thinking of this quilt as a subway map in the sky.

None of these star blocks touch each other, so choose any stars you like, without worrying about corner or edge seams colliding. To maximize motion, mix up spin directions in the blocks.

I started this quilt by pulling yellow, turquoise, aqua, teal, and white fabrics from my stash and scraps. I was conscious of choosing an array of solids and near-solids. I also made a trip or two to a quilt shop, where I bought fat quarters. Small quantities of many fabrics are better than large quantities of a few.

Quilt Top

36 star blocks
Setting shapes
- 48 squares
- 46 triangles
Finished size: 64" x 72" (162.6 x 182.9 cm)

Fabrics
- Scraps and fat quarters of yellow, turquoise, aqua, teal, and white prints, solids, and near-solids
- 2 yards (1.8m) solid deep navy blue fabric
- 2 yards (1.8m) solid dark blue fabric
- 2 yards (1.8m) solid medium-value blue fabric

Star Patterns:
- Star 4: page 75
- Star 5: page 76
- Star 6: page 76
- Star 7: page 77
- Star 8: page 77
- Star 10: page 78
- Star 11: page 79
- Star 12: page 79
- Star 15: page 81
- Star 21: page 84
- Star 24: page 85
- Star 28: page 87
- Star 31: page 89
- Star 38: page 92
- Star 42: page 94
- Star 43: page 95
- Star 44: page 95
- Star 47: page 97
- Star 48: page 97
- Star 51: page 99
- Star 53: page 100
- Star 55: page 101
- Star 57: page 102
- Star 58: page 102
- Star 60: page 103
- Star 68: page 107
- Star 70: page 108
- Star 74: page 110
- Star 75: page 111
- Star 81: page 114
- Star 88: page 117
- Star 90: page 118
- Star 92: page 119
- Star 95: page 121
- Star 96: page 121
- Star 111: page 129

1. Construct thirty-six star blocks. Don't take out the cardstock yet!

2. You need forty-eight setting square templates; rotary-cut them as described on page 136, or print eight copies of that page onto cardstock, paper, or Décor Bond. Baste your assortment of fabrics to them.

3. You'll also need forty-six equilateral triangles. I mixed up the same colors used for the squares and added a few more. Print out three copies of page 133 onto cardstock, paper, or Décor Bond. Baste fabrics to them.

4. Join the star blocks and squares first. On a design wall or floor, arrange the star blocks and squares.

Hand- or machine-stitch them together, one by one. Any piecing order works. However you decide to join them, it's going to get more awkward as the piece grows!

5. I saved the equilateral triangles for last, distributing the colors randomly. When finished, I had a gigantic, stiff star map with the templates still inside.

6. Prepare to appliqué: decide if you want to turn under and glue the protruding tails now, or if you'd prefer to do it as you sew (see page 32).

7. Remove all templates from the star blocks, squares, and triangles (unless you used Décor Bond).

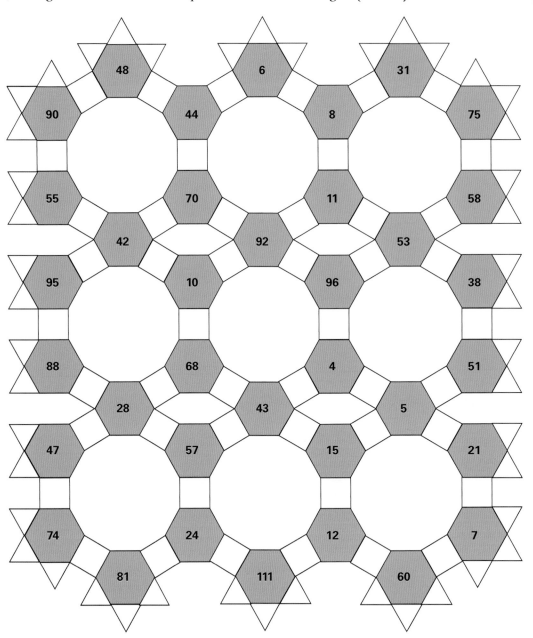

8. Construct a background. Cut the middle piece down to 15½" x 72" (39.4 x 182.9cm) so it will finish at 15" (38.1cm). Cut the side pieces down to 26" x 72" (66 x 182.9cm). Stitch the three together as shown, using a ¼" (0.65cm) seam allowance.

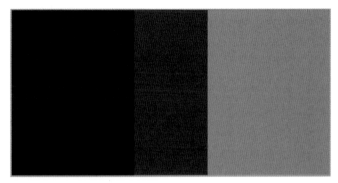

Background pieces

9. Find the center. I folded my background vertically and horizontally, finger-pressed small creases, and then crossed pins in the dead center.

Add pins to the center.

10. Lay the background on a large clean surface. Tape the corners and some edges so it's not wrinkly, but it doesn't have to be very taut.

11. Bring over the star network and smooth it on top. Start by placing the middle opening over the central marking pins. The squares and star blocks surrounding the middle opening will help you shift the grouping to the center. A yardstick (meter stick) will help you align the shapes correctly.

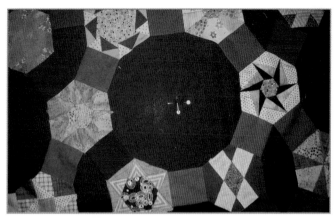

Center your hexagon star patterns over the background fabric.

12. There are other landmarks that will help with alignment. The magenta circles in the diagram below show that the small openings should have the two background fabrics meeting in the center. Star blocks under the green circles should also line up with the background fabric intersections. Pin- or hand-baste as you smooth the appliqué in position.

13. When everything is securely pinned and/or thread-basted, appliqué the network in position. I did this by machine with invisible monofilament thread. If you didn't hide the tails in advance, do it now. If sewing by machine, you need to stitch in the same direction that the tails point (see page 37).

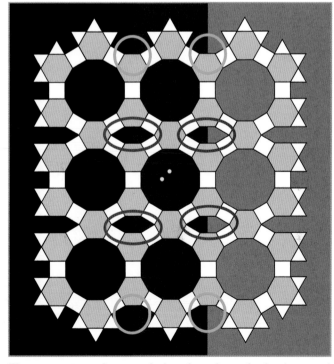

The magenta and green circles show how the background fabrics and hexagon appliqué line up.

Quilting Ideas

First, quilt "in the ditch" around the entire formation, as well as inside each large opening.

Next, I used a chalk pencil and ruler to create stars within the large openings, often by connecting points on surrounding shapes. I used single and double lines to mark different areas, which were then filled with a variety of free-motion quilting motifs.

1. Draw a flower with petals that touch the four seams shown.

2. Inspired by Star 43, start with a hexagon in the middle and then draw points to the centers of the squares.

3. Draw a six-pointed star in the middle and lines from its tips to neighboring hexagons.

4. Draw a five-pointed star, connect the points to make a pentagon surrounding it, and then draw random lines around the outside.

5. Draw a six-pointed star with tips that point to the center of the neighboring hexagons. Draw a large circle and then draw twelve points coming from it to touch the centers of all of the surrounding shapes.

6. Draw a couple of squares, and then a circle, and fill in with shapes.

7. Based on Star 72, draw a square in the middle and then draw points touching surrounding shapes as shown.

8. Draw a triangle in the center and lines to the surrounding seams.

9. Draw an octagon in the middle and eight points to the seams or centers of surrounding shapes.

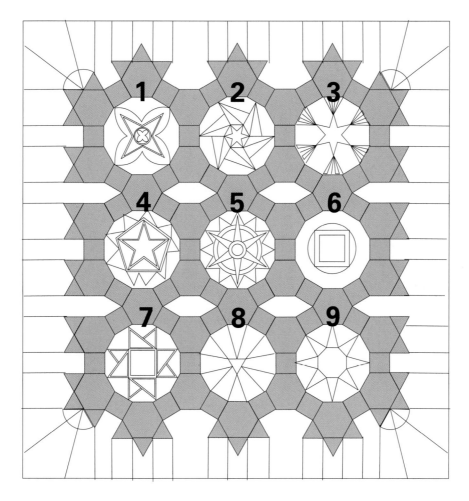

Free Luncheon Leftovers

This project started when I realized I would have leftover blocks from the Star Chart quilt (see page 65). I went through my vintage linen and quilt block collections—meaning quilt blocks NOT made by me—and pulled out everything with a compatible color scheme.

1. I pinned a tablecloth to my design wall and then did a bunch of tests pinning the blocks (with the cardstock still inside) in different arrangements. My first idea was to arrange them in some kind of hexagon, as in Tests 1 and 2. Then I tested a square arrangement and liked it far better, so I went with that.

Test 1

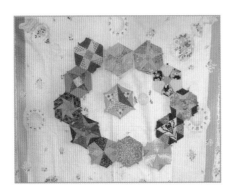

Test 2

22 stars
Finished size: 68" x 76"
(172.7 x 193.05cm)

Fabrics:
- Various vintage linens
- Enough fabric to make the stars

Star Patterns:
- Star 1: page 74
- Star 12: page 79
- Star 18: page 82
- Star 33: page 90
- Star 34: page 90
- Star 35: page 91
- Star 36: page 91
- Star 39: page 93
- Star 41: page 94
- Star 63: page 105
- Star 66: page 106
- Star 82: page 114
- Star 83: page 115
- Star 87: page 117
- Star 89: page 118
- Star 96: page 121
- Star 99: page 123
- Star 100: page 123
- Star 103: page 125
- Star 106: page 126
- Star 111: page 129

2. The next step was to piece together the background. The annotation below shows what kinds of fabrics went into the background. Everything marked "old" was collected at flea markets and thrift shops. Because dinner napkins and the like come in sets, I was able to repeat most of the elements at least once in the border.

3. When the background was assembled, I appliquéd the new blocks in position by machine with monofilament invisible thread. Directions for appliqué are on pages 36–38. In some cases, like in the upper left corner, I appliquéd the block onto a small linen first and then stitched that to a piece of plain white fabric that I'd pieced in place to serve as a placeholder.

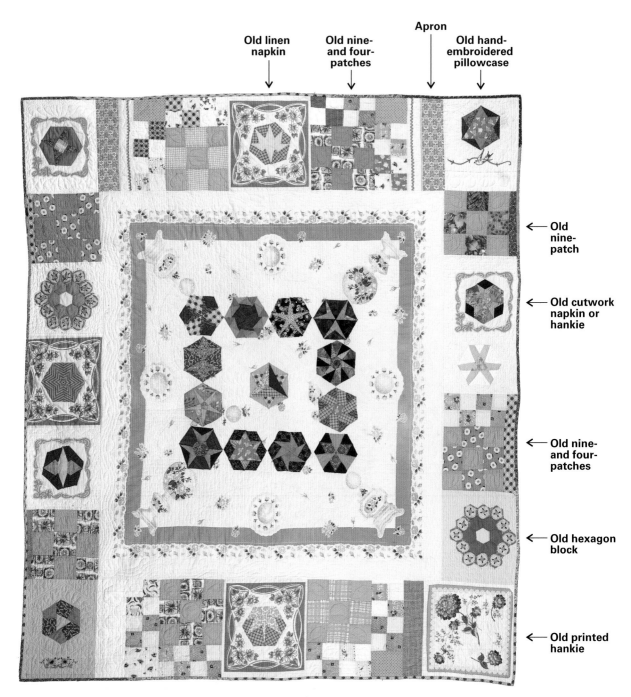

This photo displays the different types of vintage linens I used for this project.

4. Once all of the star blocks were stitched down, I added the quilt batting and backing. Just for fun, I pieced together more vintage linens for the back (though I didn't add more star blocks to the back).

I pieced the backing from more vintage linens.

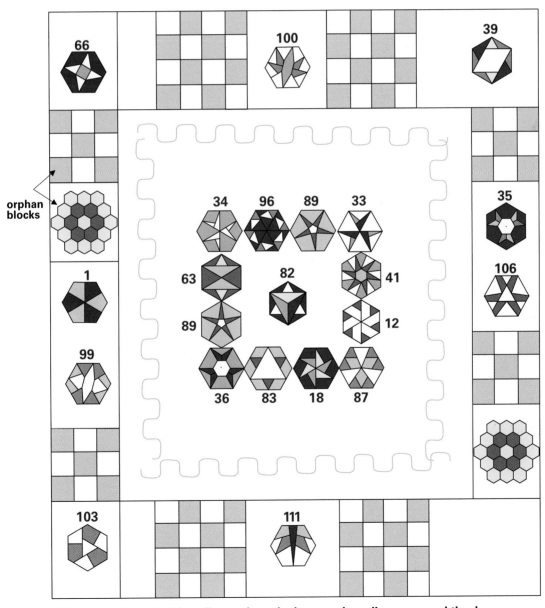

orphan blocks

The extra shapes in this quilt—such as the large and small squares and tiny hexagon pieces in the border—can be any size or design of your choosing.

Star 1

Stitch three A pieces together. Stitch another three A pieces together. Join the halves. Variation: You can easily appliqué a shape (hexagon, pentagon, square, circle) to the middle.

Front

On point

Star 1
A

Star 1
A

Star 1
A

Star 1
A

Star 1
A

Star 1
A

Star 2

Stitch three A pieces together. Stitch another three A's together. Join the halves.

Front

On point

Star 2
A

Star 2
A

Star 2
A

Star 2
A

Star 2
A

Star 2
A

74

Star 3

Stitch each A "petal" around the central hexagon. Stitch the seams that go outward from the central hexagon.

Front

A A
A B A
A A

On point

Star 3
A

Star 3
A

Star 3
A

Star 3
B
.

Star 3
A

Star 3
A

Star 3
A

Star 4

Stitch each piece B to a D. Surround the central hexagon, alternating each A with a DB unit. Stitch the seams that go outward from the central hexagon.

Front

A D B
B C A
D A D
B

On point

Star 4
D

Star 4
A

Star 4
B

Star 4
B

Star 4
A

Star 4
C
.

Star 4
D

Star 4
D

Star 4
A

Star 4
B

75

Star 5 C
Star 5 B
Star 5 A
Star 5 A
Star 5 C
Star 5 B
Star 5 B
Star 5 A
Star 5 C

Star 5

Stitch each piece B to each C. Sew one BC unit between two A pieces to make one half. To make the other half, sew one A between two BC units. Join the halves.

Front

On point

Star 6 C
Star 6 D
Star 6 B
Star 6 A
Star 6 D
Star 6 A
Star 6 B
Star 6 C
Star 6 A
Star 6 B
Star 6 A
Star 6 C
Star 6 D

Star 6

Referring to the front view below, stitch each piece C to the top of a B. Sew each BC unit to a D. Sew one BCD unit between two A pieces. Sew the two remaining BCD units on both sides of the remaining piece A. Join the halves.

Front

On point

Star 7

You can make the A diamonds from one to six different fabrics! Sew three A pieces together. Sew the remaining three into a second unit. Stitch the two units together along the straight midline. Inset the B pieces.

Front

On point

Star 8

Stitch each A to surround hexagon C. Stitch outward along the seams between the A pieces. At the end of each seam, stitch outward along the bottom of a B piece (so you don't have to cut threads.) Last, stitch the remaining AB seams.

Front

On point

Star 7
B

Star 7
B

Star 7
A

Star 7
A

Star 7
B

Star 7
A

Star 7
A

Star 7
B

Star 7
B

Star 7
A

Star 7
A

Star 7
B

Star 8
B

Star 8
A

Star 8
A

Star 8
B

Star 8
A

Star 8
C

Star 8
A

Star 8
B

Star 8
A

Star 8
A

Star 8
B

77

Star 9
B

Star 9
A

Star 9
B

Star 9
A

Star 9
A

Star 9
B

Star 9
B

Star 9
C
.

Star 9
A

Star 9
A

Star 9
B

Star 9
A

Star 9
B

Star 9

Stitch the A pieces around
C. Inset the B pieces.
Note: Star 10 is similar but has
seams in the corners.

Front

B | A | B
A | | A
B | C | B
A | | A
B | A | B

On point

Star 10
B

Star 10
A

Star 10
A

Star 10
B

Star 10
B

Star 10
A

Star 10
A

Star 10
C
.

Star 10
A

Star 10
B

Star 10
B

Star 10
A

Star 10
A

Star 10
B

Star 10

Stitch the A pieces around
C. Inset the B pieces.
Note: Star 9 is similar to this but does
not have seams in the corners.

Front

B | A
B | | A
A | C | A
B | | B
A | B

On point

78

Star 11

Sew each A to a B. Sew three AB triangles together to make a half-block. Sew the remaining three AB units together to make the other half. Sew halves together.
Note: The mirror image of this block is Star 12, below.

Front

On point

Star 12

Sew each piece A to a B. Sew three AB triangles together to make a half-block. Sew the remaining three AB units together to make the other half. Sew halves together.
Note: The mirror image of this block is Star 12, above.

Front

On point

Star 11 B
Star 11 A
Star 11 B
Star 11 A
Star 11 B
Star 11 A
Star 11 B
Star 11 A
Star 11 A
Star 11 B
Star 11 A
Star 11 B

Star 12 B
Star 12 A
Star 12 B
Star 12 A
Star 12 B
Star 12 A
Star 12 A
Star 12 B
Star 12 A
Star 12 A
Star 12 B
Star 12 B

Star 13
B

Star 13
A

Star 13
B

Star 13
A

Star 13
A

Star 13
B

Star 13
C
•

Star 13
B

Star 13
A

Star 13
A

Star 13
B

Star 13
B

Star 13
A

Star 13

Sew the A pieces around the central hexagon, C. Inset the B pieces. Note: The mirror image of this block is Star 14, below.

Front

On point

Star 14
B

Star 14
A

Star 14
B

Star 14
A

Star 14
B

Star 14
C
•

Star 14
A

Star 14
A

Star 14
B

Star 14
B

Star 14
A

Star 14

Sew the A pieces around the central hexagon, C. Inset the B pieces. Note: The mirror image of this block is Star 13, above.

Front

On point

Star 15

Sew all B pieces to A pieces. Stitch each AB unit consecutively around the central hexagon, C. Stitch seams between the AB units. Note: The mirror image of this block is Star 16, below.

Front

On point

Star 15 B

Star 15 B

Star 15 A

Star 15 A

Star 15 B

Star 15 C •

Star 15 B

Star 15 A

Star 15 A

Star 15 A

Star 15 B

Star 15 B

Star 16

Sew all B pieces to A pieces. Stitch each AB unit around the central hexagon. Stitch seams between the AB units. Note: The mirror image of this block is Star 15, above.

Front

On point

Star 16 B

Star 16 B

Star 16 A

Star 16 A

Star 16 B

Star 16 C •

Star 16 A

Star 16 A

Star 16 A

Star 16 B

Star 16 B

81

Star 17
B

Star 17
B

Star 17
A

Star 17
A

Star 17
B →

Star 17
A →

Star 17
A ←

Star 17
B ←

Star 17
A

Star 17
A

Star 17
B →

Star 17
B

Star 17

Join each piece A to the B on top of it. Sew a group of three AB units together, to make a half block. Join the other group of three to make the other half. Join the halves. Note: The mirror image of this block is Star 18, below.

Front

On point

Star 18
B

Star 18
B

Star 18
A

Star 18
A

Star 18
A →

Star 18
A ←

Star 18
B →

Star 18
B ←

Star 18
A

Star 18
A

Star 18
B

Star 18
B

Star 18

Join each piece A to the B on top of it. Sew a group of three AB units together to make a half-block. Join the other group of three to make the other half. Join the halves. Note: The mirror image of this block is Star 17, above.

Front

On point

82

Star 19

Join each piece A to the B on top of it. Stitch a group of three AB units together to make a half-block. Join the other group of three to make the other half. Stitch the halves together. Note: The mirror image of this block is Star 20, below.

Front

On point

Star 20

Join each piece A to the B on top of it. Stitch a group of three AB units together to make a half-block. Join the other group of three to make the other half. Stitch the halves together. Note: The mirror image of this block is Star 19, above.

Front

On point

Star 19 B
Star 19 B
Star 19 A
Star 19 A
Star 19 B
Star 19 A
Star 19 B
Star 19 A
Star 19 A
Star 19 A
Star 19 B

Star 20 B
Star 20 B
Star 20 A
Star 20 B
Star 20 A
Star 20 A
Star 20 A
Star 20 B
Star 20 B

83

Star 21
B

Star 21
B

Star 21
A

Star 21
A

Star 21
B

Star 21
A

Star 21
C
.

Star 21
A

Star 21
B

Star 21
A

Star 21
A

Star 21
B

Star 21
B

Star 21

Stitch each piece A to each B. Stitch each AB unit to hexagon C, along the bottom of A. Sew seams between AB units. Note: The mirror image of this block is Star 22, below. Stars 23 and 24 are variations of Stars 21 and 22, except 23 and 24 have seams in the corners.

Front

On point

Star 22
B

Star 22
B

Star 22
A

Star 22
A

Star 22
B

Star 22
B

Star 22
A

Star 22
C
.

Star 22
A

Star 22
A

Star 22
A

Star 22
B

Star 22
B

Star 22

Stitch each piece A to each B. Stitch each AB unit to hexagon C, along the bottom of A. Sew seams between AB units. Note: The mirror image of this block is Star 21, above. Stars 23 and 24 are variations of Stars 21 and 22, except 23 and 24 have seams in the corners.

Front

On point

84

Star 23

Stitch each A to a B on top of it. Stitch each AB unit to central hexagon C. Stitch seams between AB units. Note: The mirror image of this block is Star 24, below. Stars 23 and 24 are variations of Stars 21 and 22, except 23 and 24 have seams in the corners.

Front

On point

Star 23 B

Star 23 B

Star 23 A

Star 23 A

Star 23 A

Star 23 B

Star 23 C

Star 23 B

Star 23 A

Star 23 A

Star 23 A

Star 23 B

Star 23 B

Star 24

Stitch each piece A to a B on top of it. Stitch each AB unit to hexagon C. Sew seams between AB units. Note: The mirror image of this block is Star 23, above. Stars 23 and 24 are variations of Stars 21 and 22, except 23 and 24 have seams in the corners.

Front

On point

Star 24 B

Star 24 A

Star 24 B

Star 24 B

Star 24 A

Star 24 A

Star 24 C

Star 24 A

Star 24 A

Star 24 A

Star 24 B

Star 24 B

Star 24 B

85

Star 25
B

Star 25
B

Star 25
A

Star 25
A

Star 25
B

Star 25
A

Star 25
C

Star 25
B

Star 25
A

Star 25
A

Star 25
A

Star 25
B

Star 25
B

Star 25

Stitch each piece A to the B on top of it. Stitch each AB unit to surround C, along A's short edge. Sew the seams between AB units. Note: The mirror image of this block is Star 26, below.

Front

On point

Star 26
B

Star 26
A

Star 26
B

Star 26
B

Star 26
A

Star 26
C

Star 26
A

Star 26
A

Star 26
B

Star 26
B

Star 26
A

Star 26
B

Star 26

Stitch each piece A to the B on top of it. Stitch each AB unit to C along A's short edge. Sew the seams between AB units. Note: The mirror image of this block is Star 25, above.

Front

On point

86

Star 27

Stitch each piece A to the central hexagon, C. Inset the B pieces.

Front

B B
A A
A A
B B
A A
B B

On point

Star 27 **B**

Star 27 **A**

Star 27 **B**

Star 27 **A**

Star 27 **A**

Star 27 **B**

Star 27 **C** ·

Star 27 **B**

Star 27 **A**

Star 27 **A**

Star 27 **B**

Star 27 **A**

Star 27 **B**

Star 28

Stitch each piece A to the central hexagon, C. Inset the B pieces.

Front

B B
A A
B C B
A A
B B

On point

Star 28 **B**

Star 28 **A**

Star 28 **A**

Star 28 **B**

Star 28 **B**

Star 28 **A**

Star 28 **C** ·

Star 28 **A**

Star 28 **B**

Star 28 **A**

Star 28 **A**

Star 28 **B**

Star 28 **B**

87

Star 29
B

Star 29
A

Star 29
B

Star 29
B

Star 29
A

Star 29
A

Star 29
B

Star 29
C

Star 29
A

Star 29
B

Star 29
A

Star 29
A

Star 29
B

Star 29
B

Star 29

Stitch each piece A to piece C, going all the way around the central hexagon. Inset the B pieces. Note: The mirror image of this block is Star 30, below.

Front

On point

Star 30
B

Star 30
A

Star 30
A

Star 30
B

Star 30
B

Star 30
C

Star 30
A

Star 30
A

Star 30
A

Star 30
B

Star 30
B

Star 30
A

Star 30
B

Star 30

Stitch each piece A to piece C, going all the way around the central hexagon. Inset the B pieces. Note: The mirror image of this block is Star 29, above.

Front

On point

88

Star 31

Sew the six A pieces to surround piece C. Inset the B pieces.

Front

B B
A
B A A B
C
B A A B
A
B B

On point

Star 31 B

Star 31 B

Star 31 A

Star 31 A

Star 31 C
.

Star 31 B →

← Star 31 B

Star 31 A

Star 31 A

Star 31 A

Star 31 A

Star 31 B

Star 31 B

Star 32

Sew six A pieces to surround piece C. Inset the B pieces.

Front

B
B A A B
A C A
B A A B
B

On point

Star 32 B

Star 32 B

Star 32 A

Star 32 A

Star 32 B

Star 32 A

Star 32 C
.

Star 32 A

Star 32 B

Star 32 A

Star 32 A

Star 32 B

Star 32 B

Star 33
C

Star 33
B

Star 33
A

Star 33
D

Star 33
D

Star 33
A

Star 33
A

Star 33
B

Star 33
C

Star 33
C

Star 33
B

Star 33
D

Star 33

Stitch each B to a C. Stitch each A to a CB unit. Make three ABC units. Stitch one ABC between two Ds. Stitch the other D between two ABC units. Stitch the block halves together. Note: This star and Star 34 are variations of one another. Star 33 has corner seams; Star 34 doesn't.

Front

C
B
A
D
D
B
A
A
C
C
D

On point

Star 34

Stitch each B to a C. Stitch each A to a CB unit. Make three ABC units. Stitch one ABC unit between two D pieces. Stitch the other D between two ABC units. Stitch the block halves together. Note: This star and Star 33 are variations of one another: Star 33 has corner seams; Star 34 doesn't.

Star 34
D

Star 34
C

Star 34
B

Star 34
A

Star 34
B

Star 34
A

Star 34
C

Star 34
D

Star 34
A

Star 34
B

Star 34
C

Star 34
D

Front

C
D
B
A
A
B
D
C
A
B
C
D

On point

Star 35

Join each A to a B. Inset the E pieces in each AB unit. Surround the central hexagon with D pieces, alternating with the ABE units. Finally, stitch the seams joining each D to an ABE unit. Note: This star and Star 36 are variations of one another. This star doesn't have corner seams.

Front

D E
A
B
E C D
B
A
D E

On point

Star 35 E

Star 35 D

Star 35 B
Star 35 A

Star 35 C
·

Star 35 A
Star 35 E
Star 35 B

Star 35 D

Star 35 B
Star 35 A
Star 35 E
Star 35 D

Star 36

Join each A to a B. Inset the E pieces in each AB unit. Surround the central hexagon with D pieces, alternating with the ABE units. Finally, stitch the seams joining each D to an ABE unit. Note: This star and Star 35 are variations of one another. This star has corner seams.

Front

E
B A
D D
C
E B A
E B
D

On point

Star 36 E

Star 36 A
Star 36 B

Star 36 D

Star 36 C
·

Star 36 D

Star 36 B
Star 36 A
Star 36 E

Star 36 A
Star 36 B
Star 36 E

Star 36 D

Star 37

Star 37
E

Star 37
A

Star 37
B

Star 37
D

Star 37
D

Star 37
C
.

Star 37
B

Star 37
A

Star 37
E

Star 37
A

Star 37
D

Star 37
B

Star 37
E

A and B are mirror images of one another. Each has four edges, one of which is short. Baste fabric tightly, even against the short edge. Glue-basting works best. D and E are identical; they have different letters if you want to alternate colors. Make three AEB units. Stitch D pieces, alternating with AEB units to surround the central hexagon. Sew seams between D pieces and AEB units. Note: This star and Star 38 are variations of one another. This star doesn't have corner seams.

Front

On point

Star 38

Star 38
E

Star 38
B

Star 38
A

Star 38
D

Star 38
A

Star 38
D

Star 38
C
.

Star 38
E

Star 38
B

Star 38
B

Star 38
D

Star 38
E

Star 38
A

A and B are mirror images of one another. Each has four edges, one of which is short. Baste fabric tightly, even against the short edge. Glue basting works best. Stitch three AEB units. Stitch D pieces, alternating with AEB units, around the central hexagon. Sew seams between the D pieces and the AEB units. Note: This star and Star 37 are variations of one another. This star has corner seams.

Front

On point

Star 39

Stitch each A to a D. Attach the two AD units to opposite sides of C, the central diamond. Stitch each B to a D. Attach each BD unit to the remaining sides.

Front

On point

Star 40

Go around the center piece, joining pieces D, B, A, I, G, H, K, and E. Inset pieces F and J. Sew out the seams, emanating from piece C. When this star is on point, it doesn't make a lot of sense, but when the jewel in the center is straight up (with the bottom of piece C pointing straight down), it looks like a glowing diamond.

Front

On point

Star 39
A

Star 39
B

Star 39
D

Star 39
D

Star 39
C

Star 39
D

Star 39
D

Star 39
A

Star 39
B

Star 40
F

Star 40
A

Star 40
B

Star 40
D

Star 40
E

Star 40
C

Star 40
I

Star 40
G

Star 40
H

Star 40
K

Star 40
J

93

Star 41 (diagram labels)

Star 41 B
Star 41 D
Star 41 B
Star 41 D
Star 41 A
Star 41 A
Star 41 D
Star 41 A
Star 41 B
Star 41
C .
Star 41 B
Star 41 D
Star 41 A
Star 41 A
Star 41 A
Star 41 D
Star 41 B
Star 41 D
Star 41 B

Star 41

Referring to the front diagram, sew each A surrounding the central hexagon, C. Sew each B to a D. Inset each BD unit between the star points. Note: The mirror image of this block is Star 42, below.

Front

On point

Star 42 (diagram labels)

Star 42 B
Star 42 D
Star 42 B
Star 42 D
Star 42 A
Star 42 A
Star 42 D
Star 42 A
Star 42 B
Star 42
C .
Star 42 B
Star 42 A
Star 42 A
Star 42 D
Star 42 A
Star 42 D
Star 42 D
Star 42 B
Star 42 B

Star 42

Referring to the front view diagram, sew each A surrounding C. Sew each D to a B. Inset each DB unit between the star points. Note: The mirror image of this block is Star 41, above.

Front

On point

Star 43

Stitch pieces ABD together. Repeat five times. Stitch the base of each piece A (its shortest side) all the way around piece C. Stitch out the emanating lines. Note: The mirror image of this block is Star 44, below.

Front

On point

Star 43 D
Star 43 D
Star 43 B
Star 43 A
Star 43 B
Star 43 A
Star 43 D
Star 43 B
Star 43 A
Star 43 D
Star 43 B
Star 43 A

Star 43
C
.

Star 43 A
Star 43 B
Star 43 D
Star 43 A
Star 43 B
Star 43 D

Star 44

Stitch pieces ABD together. Repeat five times. Stitch the base of each piece A (its shortest side) all the way around piece C. Stitch out the emanating line. Note: The mirror image of this block is Star 43, above.

Front

On point

Star 44 D
Star 44 B
Star 44 A
Star 44 D
Star 44 B
Star 44 D
Star 44 B
Star 44 A

Star 44
C
.

Star 44 A
Star 44 B
Star 44 A
Star 44 B
Star 44 D
Star 44 A
Star 44 B
Star 44 D
Star 44 D

Star 45

Join piece A to B and D. Repeat five times. Attach the six ABD units to the central hexagon. Stitch the outward lines between the units. Note: The mirror image of this block is Star 46, below.

Front

On point

Star 46

Join each piece A to a B and D. Make six ABD units. Attach the ABD units to the central hexagon. Stitch outward seams between units. Note: The mirror image of this block is Star 45, above.

Front

On point

Star 45 D

Star 45 D

Star 45 A

Star 45 B

Star 45 D

Star 45 B

Star 45 A

Star 45 A

Star 45 B

Star 45 D

Star 45
C
.

Star 45 D

Star 45 B

Star 45 A

Star 45 A

Star 45 B

Star 45 A

Star 45 B

Star 45 D

Star 45 D

Star 46 D

Star 46 B

Star 46 A

Star 46 A

Star 46 B

Star 46 D

Star 46 D

Star 46 B

Star 46 A

Star 46 D

Star 46
C
.

Star 46 A

Star 46 B

Star 46 A

Star 46 A

Star 46 B

Star 46 B

Star 46 D

Star 46 D

96

Star 47

These B pieces are very small. I recommend glue-basting them. Join the B pieces to the C pieces, and then join the A pieces to the BC units. Make six ABC units. Join three ABC units to form a half-block. Join the other three for the other half. Join the halves. This star has no corner seams, unlike Star 48, below.

Front

On point

Star 47 C

Star 47 C

Star 47 B

Star 47 B

Star 47 A

Star 47 A

Star 47 B

Star 47 C

Star 47 C

Star 47 A

Star 47 A

Star 47 B

Star 47 B

Star 47 A

Star 47 A

Star 47 B

Star 47 C

Star 47 C

Star 48

These B pieces are very small. I recommend glue-basting them. Join the B pieces to the C pieces, and then join the A pieces to the BC units. Make six ABC units. Join three ABC units to form a half-block. Join the other three for the other half. Join the halves. This star has corner seams, unlike Star 47, above.

Front

On point

Star 48 C

Star 48 B

Star 48 B

Star 48 C

Star 48 C

Star 48 A

Star 48 A

Star 48 B

Star 48 A

Star 48 B

Star 48 A

Star 48 A

Star 48 A

Star 48 C

Star 48 B

Star 48 B

Star 48 C

Star 48 C

97

Star 49
D

Star 49
B

Star 49
A

Star 49
D

Star 49
A

Star 49
B

Star 49
D

Star 49
B

Star 49
A

Star 49
C
·

Star 49
A

Star 49
B

Star 49
D

Star 49
A

Star 49
B

Star 49
D

Star 49
B

Star 49
A

Star 49
D

Star 49

Working from the front, join each A to the B on its right. Attach the six AB units to the central hexagon. Stitch the remaining seams between the A pieces and B pieces. Inset the D pieces.

Front

On point

Star 50
C

Star 50
B

Star 50
A

Star 50
C

Star 50
B

Star 50
A

Star 50
C

Star 50
A

Star 50
B

Star 50
A

Star 50
A

Star 50
C

Star 50
A

Star 50
B

Star 50
C

Star 50

Join each A to each B, with B on top. Sew three AB units together to make a half-star. Sew the other three together. Join the halves. Inset the C pieces.

Front

On point

Star 51

Referring to the diagram, surround C with its neighbors in sequence. Start at the top center. Attach pieces B, A, D, A, B, A, D, and A. Inset remaining pieces E, F, G, and H. My version, in the photo, uses the same fabric for the E, F, G, and H pieces.

Front

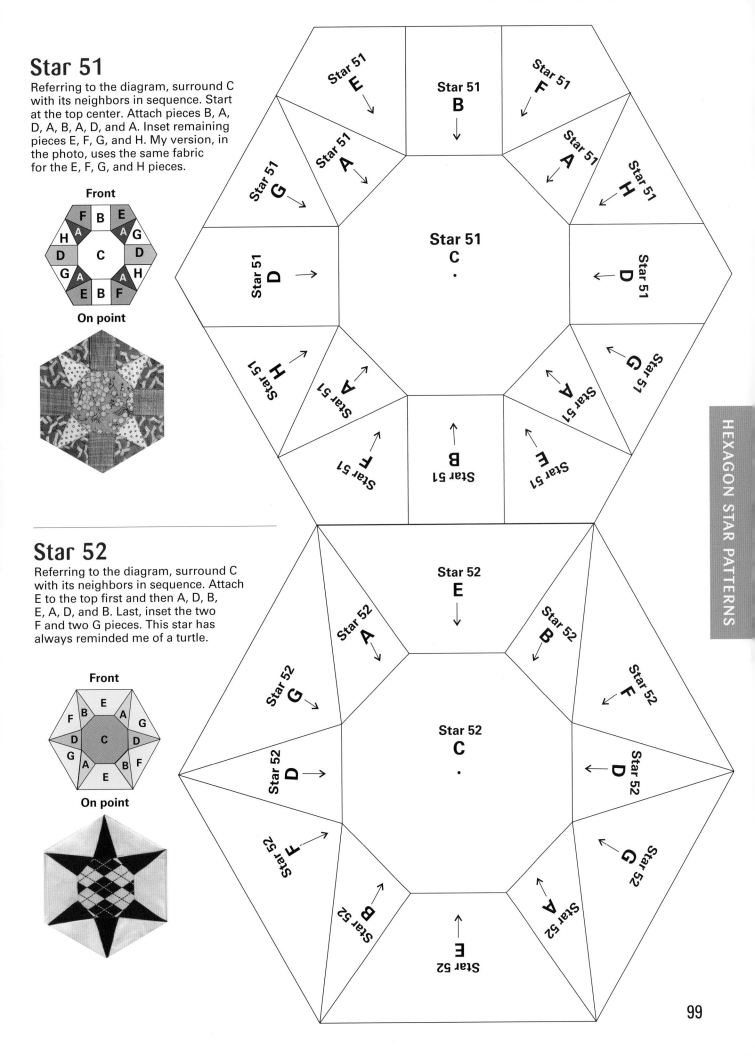

On point

Star 52

Referring to the diagram, surround C with its neighbors in sequence. Attach E to the top first and then A, D, B, E, A, D, and B. Last, inset the two F and two G pieces. This star has always reminded me of a turtle.

Front

On point

Star 51 E

Star 51 B

Star 51 F

Star 51 A

Star 51 G

Star 51 A

Star 51 H

Star 51 C

Star 51 D

Star 51 D

Star 51 H

Star 51 A

Star 51 G

Star 51 A

Star 51 F

Star 51 B

Star 51 E

Star 52 E

Star 52 A

Star 52 B

Star 52 G

Star 52 F

Star 52 D

Star 52 C

Star 52 D

Star 52 F

Star 52 G

Star 52 B

Star 52 A

Star 52 E

99

Star 53
D

Star 53
E

Star 53
B

Star 53
C
•

Star 53
A

Star 53
A

Star 53
B

Star 53
E

Star 53
D

Star 53

Join each A to a B. Join each D to an E. Sew the units surrounding the central square. Variation: Cross out the lines between the A and B pieces, and between the D and E pieces. There will be only four "petals."

Front

On point

Star 54
A1

Star 54
B6

Star 54
B1

Star 54
A6

Star 54
A2

Star 54
B5

Star 54
C
•

Star 54
B2

Star 54
A5

Star 54
A3

Star 54
B4

Star 54
B3

Star 54
A4

Star 54

For fan "blades," use 2–12 fabrics. (I used three: light, medium, and dark. I made two dark A's, two medium A's, and two light A's. Same with the B's.) Join A's and B's into pairs with a flat base (A1 to B1, A2 to B2, etc.) Make six pairs. Stitch the AB units around C. Stitch adjoining seams.

Front

B6 A1
A6 B1
B5 A2
C
A5 B2
B4 A3
A4 B3

On point

100

Star 55

Contrasting values are crucial to an intertwined illusion! Use two values for the star plus one for the background. Stitch one A to the background-colored C at its base. Repeat by stitching with the second color of A to the C at its base. Set aside. Stitch pieces D, B, and E together. Repeat to make another DBE unit. Now you have four units. Join along their long seams.

Front

On point

Star 56

For the first half, join two A pieces as shown in the diagram. Inset the B piece. Join a D to the left and an E to the right. Add a C to one side. Repeat this procedure to create the opposite half. Join the halves.

Front

On point

Star 55
C
color 3
(background)

Star 55
D
color 3
(background)

Star 55
B
color 1

Star 55
E
color 3
(background)

Star 55
A
color 2

Star 55
A
color 1

Star 55
E
color 3
(background)

Star 51
B
color 2

Star 55
D
color 3
(background)

Star 55
C
color 3
(background)

Star 56
D

Star 56
A

Star 56
C

Star 56
B

Star 56
E

Star 56
A

Star 56
A

Star 56
E

Star 56
C

Star 56
A

Star 56
B

Star 56
D

101

Star 57
A

Star 57
C →

Star 57
D ←

Star 57
B →

Star 57
B ←

Star 57
D ↗

Star 57
A ↑

Star 57
C ↖

Star 57

Referring to the diagram, join pieces A, C, B, and D, in that order. Repeat for the other half. Stitch the halves together. For a different look, make A and B from the same fabric and make the C and D pieces from a darker fabric.

Front

D	A	C
B		B
C	A	D

On point

Star 58
E

Star 58
E

Star 58
A

Star 58
D ↘

Star 58
C ↙

Star 54
B →

Star 54
B ←

Star 58
C ↗

Star 58
A ↑

Star 58
D ↖

Star 58
E ↑

Star 58
E ↑

Star 58

Referring to the diagram, sew each A between two E pieces. Surround the piece EAE units with a C on one side and a D on the other. Stitch a B piece next to the C. That makes a half-block. Repeat to create the second DEAECB unit. Stitch the halves together.

Front

E	A	E
C		D
B		B
D		C
E	A	E

On point

Star 59

Referring to the diagram, sew each piece A between a C and a D. Add a B piece to the right side of the CAD unit. Repeat to make a second CAD unit and join it to the second B piece. Join the halves.

Front

C | D
A
B | B
D | C

On point

Star 59 D ↓

Star 59 C ↓

Star 59 A ↓

Star 55 B →

Star 55 B ←

Star 59 A ↑

Star 59 C ↗

Star 59 D ↗

Star 60

Referring to the diagram, sew each piece B between a D and a C piece. Add an A piece to the right side of a DBC unit. Repeat to add an A piece to the far right of the second DBC unit. Join the halves.

Front

C | A | D
B | B
D | A | C

On point

Star 60 D ↓

Star 60 A ↓

Star 60 C ↙

Star 60 B →

Star 60 B ←

Star 60 C ↗

Star 60 A ↑

Star 60 D ↗

103

Star 61
C

Star 61
B

Star 61
B

Star 61
C

Star 61
C

Star 61
A

Star 57
A

Star 57
A

Star 61
A

Star 61
C

Star 61
C

Star 61
B

Star 61
B

Star 61
C

Star 61

The A shapes are identical, but you may want to use two different fabrics, as in the photo below. Stitch two adjoining A pieces together. Stitch the remaining A pieces together. Join the two pairs to make a large diamond. Stitch four B pieces to opposite sides of the AAAA unit. Set in the C pieces.

Front

On point

Star 62
D

Star 62
D

Star 62
C

Star 62
A1

Star 62
B1

Star 62
A2

Star 62
B2

Star 62
C

Star 62
D

Star 62
D

Star 62

Pieces A and B are identical. In the photo below, I used solid red for A1 and A2, and a print with white circles for B1 and B2. Alternative: Match B1 to A2 and use another fabric for A1 and B2. Piecing: Join A and B pieces into two pairs. Sew each C between two D pieces. Stitch a DCD unit to one AB unit. Stitch the other DCD to the other AB. Join the halves.

Front

On point

104

Star 63

Stitch a C between two D pieces. Repeat with the remaining D pieces and a C piece. Stitch a B piece to an A piece. Stitch the remaining B piece to an A piece. Join the BA units to make the central rectangle. Stitch the DCD units to opposite sides of the rectangle.

Front

On point

Star 63 **A**

Star 63 **D**

Star 63 **D**

Star 63 **C**

Star 63 **B**

Star 63 **B**

Star 63 **C**

Star 63 **D**

Star 63 **D**

Star 63 **A**

Star 64

Sew pieces A, B, A, and B surrounding the central square. Inset the D and E pieces, checking carefully against the diagram to make sure the pieces are in the correct location.

Front

On point

Star 64 **E**

Star 64 **A**

Star 64 **D**

Star 64 **B**

Star 64 **C**
•

Star 64 **B**

Star 64 **D**

Star 64 **A**

Star 64 **E**

Star 65 B

Star 65 A

Star 65 D

Star 65 C •

Star 65 D

Star 65 A

Star 65 B

Star 65

Referring to the diagram, sew each A piece to a D piece. Attach the two AD pairs to opposite sides of piece C. Inset the B pieces. Note: The more complicated mirror image of this block is Star 66, below.

Front

On point

Star 66 D

Star 66 A

Star 66 A

Star 66 C •

Star 66 B

Star 66 B

Star 66 A

Star 66 A

Star 66 D

Star 66

To make this star a complicated mirror image of Star 65 above, add two lines (in red) that create a central square. Stitch the A pieces around the central square, C. Inset pieces B and D. (Ignore the red lines if you don't want a central square; in that case, follow the piecing directions for Star 65.)

Front

On point

Star 67

Method 1: Surround piece C with D and E pieces, then inset A and B pieces.
Method 2: Join A, E, and B. Repeat with the second AEB. Join pieces DCD. Sew the three sections together.

Front

A
E D
B C B
D E
A

On point

Star 67 A

Star 67 D

Star 67 E

Star 67 B

Star 67 C •

Star 67 B

Star 67 D

Star 67 E

Star 67 A

Star 68

Method 1: Surround diamond C with D, E, D, and E in sequence. Inset A and B pieces.
Method 2: Referring to the diagram, join pieces ADB. Join the second set of pieces ADB. Join pieces ECE. Sew the three units together.

Front

A
E D
B C B
D E
A

On point

Star 68 A

Star 68 D

Star 68 E

Star 68 B

Star 68 C •

Star 68 B

Star 68 E

Star 68 D

Star 68 A

107

Star 69 E →

Star 69 D ↓

Star 69 A ↓

Star 69 F ←

Star 69 G →

Star 69 C •

Star 69 B →

Star 67 B →

Star 69 B ←

Star 69 G ←

Star 69 F ↗

Star 69 A ↑

Star 69 D ↑

Star 69 E ↗

Star 69

This is a nine-patch block. Referring to the diagram, join each A piece to a D piece. Join each B to a G. Create a top horizontal row of piece F, unit DA, and piece E. Create a middle row of GB, C, and BG. The bottom row is E, AD, and F. Join the three rows along their horizontal edges. Note: The mirror image of this block is Star 70, below.

Front

F	D / A	E
G	B	C	B	G
E	A / D	F

On point

Star 70 D ↓

Star 70 F →

Star 70 A ↓

Star 70 E ←

Star 70 B →

Star 70 C •

Star 70 G ←

Star 70 G →

Star 70 B ←

Star 70 E ↗

Star 70 A ↑

Star 70 D ↓

Star 70 F ↗

Star 70

Referring to the diagram, join each A to a D. Join each B to a G. Create a top horizontal row of pieces F, AD, and F. Create a middle row of GB, C, and BG. The bottom row is F, DA, and E. Join the three rows on their long horizontal edges. Note: The mirror image of this block is Star 69, above.

Front

E	A / D	F
G	B	C	B	G
F	D / A	E

On point

Star 71

This is an abbreviated and hexagonized version of the Mariner's Star block. Attach pieces A, B, A, and B to central piece C. Stitch each D between a G and an H. Stitch each E between an F and an I. Inset the IEF and GDH units between the A and B star points.

Front

On point

Star 72

Make two DB pairs. Sew each DB to an A. Sew two GB units. Add each GB to an A piece.

Method 1: Surround C with ABD and ABG units. Inset the F and E pieces.

Method 2: Assemble the block in three vertical columns. On the left (in the diagram), stitch an E on top of a GBA. Sew an F to the bottom. In the middle column, sew unit DAB on top of C, and another ABD unit on the bottom. In the right column, sew F on top of unit ABG, and add E to the bottom. Stitch the columns together.

Front

On point

Star 71 G

Star 71 F

Star 71 A

Star 71 D

Star 71 E

Star 71 H

Star 71 I

Star 71 B

Star 71 C

Star 71 B

Star 71 I

Star 71 H

Star 71 E

Star 71 D

Star 71 A

Star 71 F

Star 71 G

Star 72 D

Star 72 B

Star 72 F

Star 72 A

Star 72 E

Star 72 A

Star 72 G

Star 72 B

Star 72 C

Star 72 B

Star 72 G

Star 72 A

Star 72 E

Star 72 A

Star 72 B

Star 72 F

Star 72 D

109

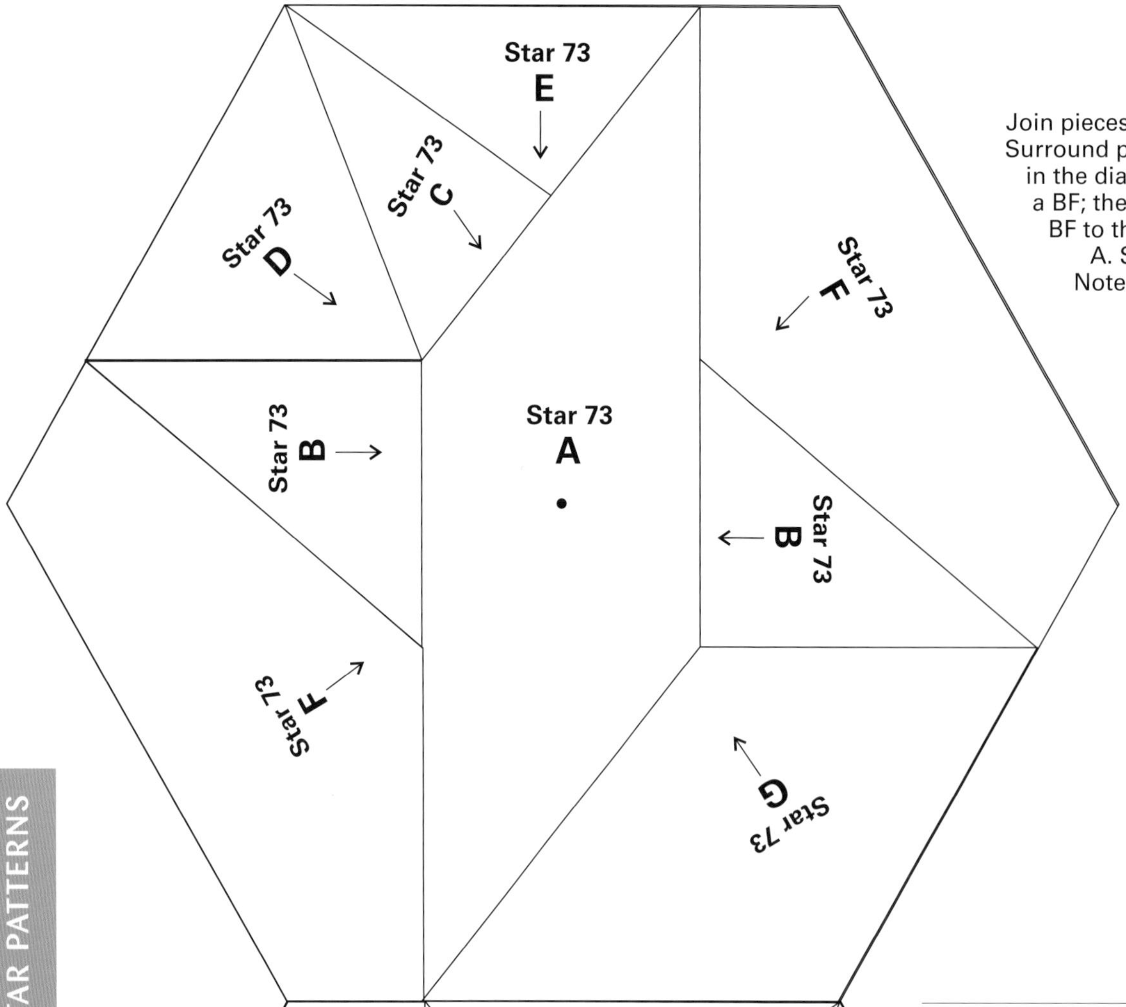

Star 73
E

Star 73
C

Star 73
D

Star 73
F

Star 73
B

Star 73
A
•

Star 73
B

Star 73
F

Star 73
G

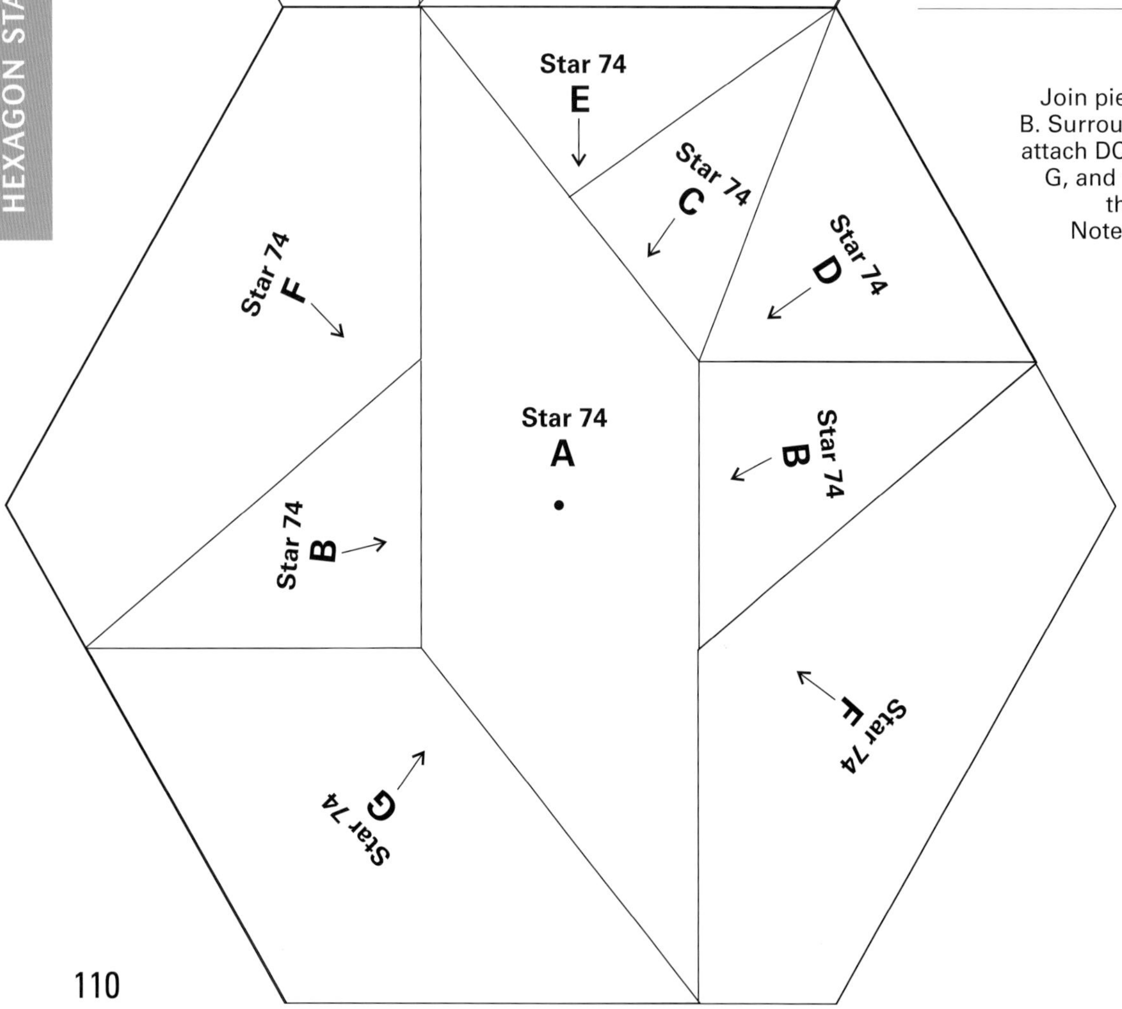

Star 73

Join pieces ECD. Join each B to an F. Surround piece A: Moving clockwise in the diagram, add ECD to A, then a BF; then a G, and finally, the last BF to the remaining open side of A. Sew the remaining seams. Note: The mirror image of this block is Star 74, below.

Front

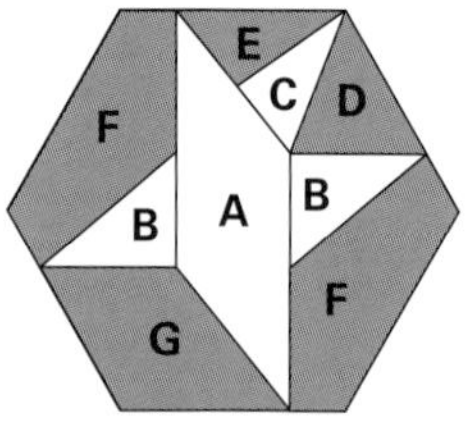

E
F C D
B A B
G F

On point

Star 74
E

Star 74
C

Star 74
D

Star 74
F

Star 74
B

Star 74
A
•

Star 74
B

Star 74
F

Star 74
G

Star 74

Join pieces DCE. Join each F to a B. Surround A with those subunits: attach DCE to A, then FB to A, then G, and then the last FB unit. Sew the seam between G and B. Note: The mirror image of this block is Star 73, above.

Front

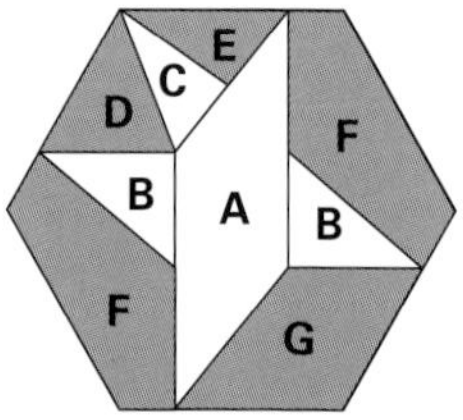

E
D C F
B A B
F G

On point

110

Star 75

This star has three vertical columns. From the front diagram, the left column from top to bottom is EDF. The middle column is BACAB. The right column is FDE. Join the AB pieces. Sew the AB units to the top and bottom of C. Join the left-column pieces EDF, and the right-column pieces FDE. Join the two sides to the central column.

Front

E B
  A F
D C D
F A E
  B

On point

Star 76

Method 1: Attach the A pieces around triangle C. Inset the B pieces.
Method 2: Sew two A pieces to the right and left of triangle C. Inset the top B. Sew two B pieces to the right and left of the remaining piece A. Sew that BAB bottom unit to the ACAB unit above it.

Front

  B
A C A
B A B

On point

Star 75 B

Star 75 A

Star 75 F

Star 75 E

Star 75 C

Star 75 D

Star 75 D

Star 75 E

Star 75 F

Star 76 A

Star 75 B

Star 76 B

Star 76 A

Star 76 A

Star 76 C

Star 76 B

Star 76 B

Star 76 A

111

Star 77

Sew piece C to its points in sequence: from the front, moving clockwise, attach H, H, F, G, and the last H to the central C piece. Then go around again, insetting the background pieces A, D, I, E, and B.

Front

On point

Star 77 **A**

Star 77 **H**

Star 77 **B**

Star 77 **H**

Star 77 **C** •

Star 77 **H**

Star 77 **D**

Star 77 **E**

Star 77 **F**

Star 77 **G**

Star 77 **I**

Star 78

Join each A to a D. Join G and H. Join E and F. Referring to the diagram, attach all of the star points, in order, to the central pentagon, C. Insert the background pieces, I, M, L, K, and J, making sure that you're placing each between the correct star points.

Front

On point

Star 78 **I**

Star 78 **A**

Star 78 **D**

Star 78 **J**

Star 78 **D**

Star 78 **A**

Star 78 **A**

Star 78 **D**

Star 78 **C** •

Star 78 **M**

Star 78 **K**

Star 78 **F**

Star 78 **E**

Star 78 **H**

Star 78 **G**

Star 78 **L**

112

Star 79

Working clockwise in the diagram, stitch pieces A, B, A, and B to the central piece C. Inset the two D and E pieces, checking that you're putting each where they belong (it's easy to mix them up!).

Front

On point

Star 79
D ↓

Star 79
A ↓

Star 79
B ↓

Star 79
E →

Star 79
C
·

← Star 79
E

Star 79
B ↑

A ↑
Star 79

D ↑
Star 79

Star 80

Referring to the diagram, sew each A piece to the top of a B. Sew each F on top of a G. Going clockwise around piece C, attach each piece in sequence: D, B, E, G, D, B, E, and G. Stitch seams outward from the center. (I like to refer to this block as "Sauron's Eye Star.")

Front

On point

Star 80
A ↓

Star 80
D ↓

Star 80
F ↓

Star 80
B ↓

Star 80
G ↓

Star 80
E →

Star 80
C
·

← Star 80
E

G ↑
Star 80

B ↑
Star 80

F ↑
Star 80

D ↑
Star 80

A ↑
Star 80

113

Star 81
B

Star 81
A

Star 81
B

Star 81
B

Star 81
A

Star 81
C
.

Star 81
B

Star 81
B

Star 81
A

Star 82
B

Star 82
C

Star 82
B

Star 82
B

Star 82
C

Star 82
A

Star 82
A

Star 82
B

Star 82
A

Star 82
B

Star 82
C

Star 82
B

Star 81

Sew each A piece between two B pieces. Then sew each BAB unit to each side of the C triangle.

Front

On point

Star 82

For an illusion of depth, use a light, medium, and dark fabric in each of the three A pieces. Join the A pieces first to form a large triangle. Stitch each C piece between two B pieces. Last, sew each BCB unit to each side of the AAA triangle.

Front

On point

114

Star 83

Sew each A piece between two B pieces. Sew each BAB unit to each side of the large C triangle.

Front

On point

Star 84

For an illusion of depth, use a light, medium, and dark fabric in each of the three A pieces. Join the A pieces first to form a large triangle. Stitch each C piece between two B pieces. Last, sew each BCB unit to each side of the central triangle.

Front

On point

Star 83 **B**

Star 83 **B**

Star 83 **A**

Star 83 **A**

Star 83 **B**

Star 83 **B**

Star 83 **C**

Star 83 **B**

Star 83 **A**

Star 83 **B**

Star 84 **B**

Star 84 **B**

Star 84 **C**

Star 84 **C**

Star 84 **B**

Star 84 **A**

Star 84 **A**

Star 84 **B**

Star 84 **A**

Star 84 **B**

Star 84 **C**

Star 84 **B**

115

Star 85 D

Star 85 B

Star 85 A

Star 85 A

Star 85 B

Star 85 C
.

Star 85 D

Star 85 D

Star 85 B

Star 85 A

Star 85

Sew each B between a piece D and A. When you have three DBA units, stitch one to each side of triangle C.

Front

A D
B   B
D   A
C
A   D
B
D

On point

Star 86 A

Star 86 B

Star 86 D

Star 86 B

Star 86 B

Star 86 D

Star 86 C
.

Star 86 A

Star 86 B

Star 86 B

Star 86 A

Star 86 B

Star 86 D

Star 86

Sew each A piece between two B pieces. Sew each BAB unit to one side of triangle C. When all three BAB units are attached, add the D pieces.

Front

D   B   A
B   B
A   C   D
B   B
D   B   A

On point

116

Star 87

Sew each A between a D and C. For the first half, sew a B between two DAC units. For the second half, sew two B pieces to both sides of a DAC unit. Join the halves.

Front

On point

Star 14
C

Star 87
D

Star 87
A

Star 87
B

Star 87
B

Star 87
D

Star 87
A

Star 87
A

Star 87
C

Star 87
C

Star 87
B

Star 87
D

Star 88

Sew each A between a B and D piece. Attach each BAD unit to each side of triangle C.

Front

On point

Star 88
B

Star 88
D

Star 88
A

Star 88
A

Star 88
C

Star 88
D

Star 88
B

Star 88
B

Star 88
A

Star 88
D

117

Star 89
B

Star 89
G

Star 89
A

Star 89
A

Star 89
A

Star 89
C

•

Star 89
D

Star 89
F

Star 89
A

Star 89
A

Star 89
E

Star 89

This block is tricky because each background piece is different. Stitch A pieces surrounding the central C pentagon. Inset the background pieces, paying attention to the diagram for correct order.

Front

On point

Star 90
I

Star 90
H

Star 90
J

Star 90
B

Star 90
A

Star 90
G

Star 90
Q

Star 90
K

Star 90
A

Star 90
A

Star 90
P

Star 90
D

Star 90
C

•

Star 90
A

Star 90
F

Star 90
L

Star 90
E

Star 90
O

Star 90
M

Star 90
N

Star 90

Be warned: this ten-point star is challenging. All pieces are different except the A pieces. Sew the five A points around piece C. Sew each background star point B, D, E, F, and G between its background neighbors (B between I and J, D between K and L, etc.) Inset the three-piece units (IBJ, KDL, MEN, etc.) between the A pieces, paying attention to order and the orientation of the central C pentagon.

Front

On point

118

Star 91

On the upper left, sew a B between a D and an F. In the upper right, sew a B between a G and an E. In the lower left, sew a B between an E and a G. In the lower right, sew a B between an F and a D. Stitch C between two A pieces. Stitch the upper left quadrant to a vertical A. Stitch the upper right quadrant to the other side of the same A. Do the bottom the same way. Sew the top portion to the top of the ACA unit and sew the bottom portion to the bottom of the ACA unit.

Front

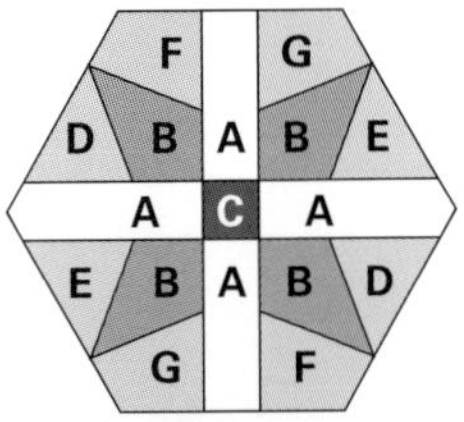

F		G
D	B	A	B	E

On point

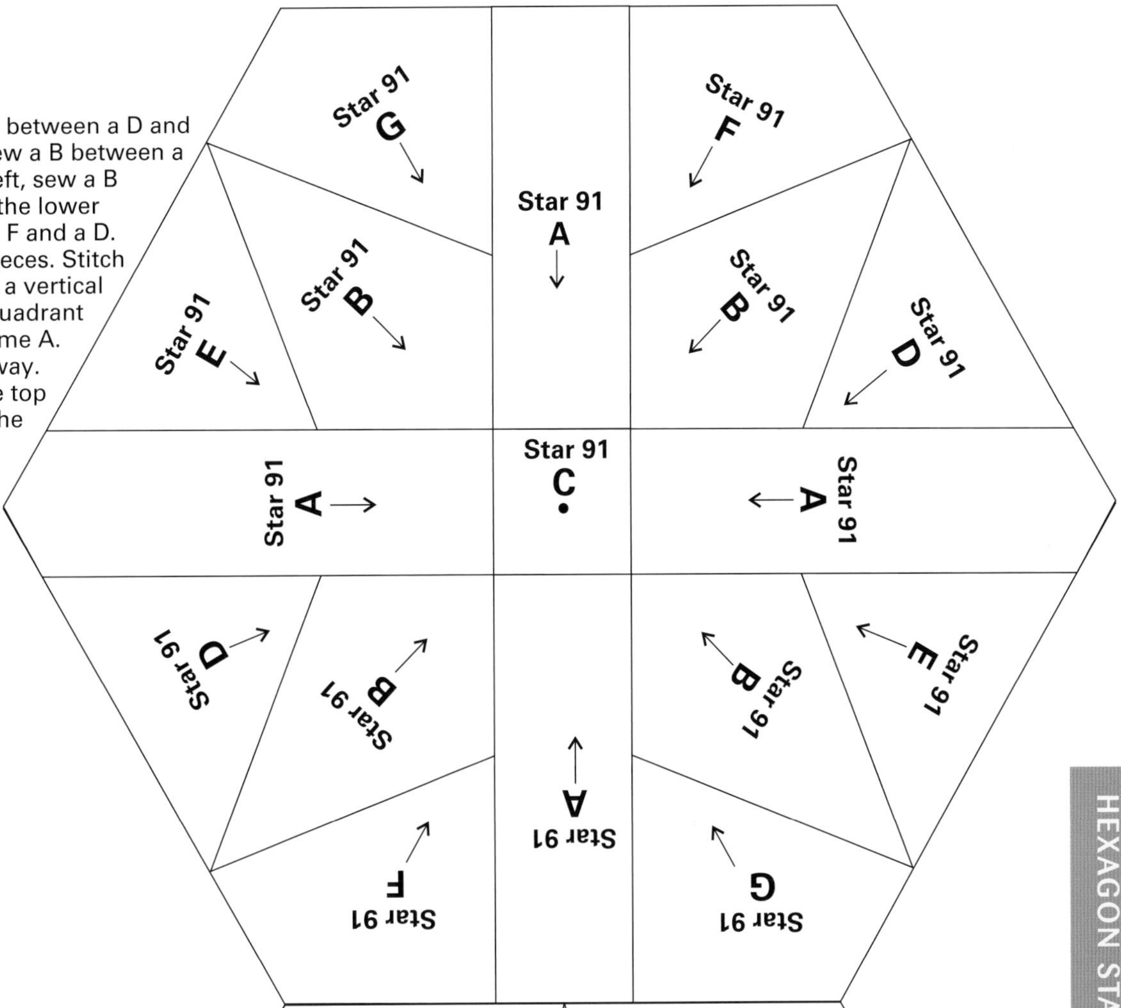

Star 92

Surround piece C with the star points in sequence. If you start with the top vertical B, moving clockwise in the diagram, add A, D, A, B, A, D, and A. Then set in the background pieces clockwise: E, G, H, F, E, G, H, F, paying attention to the arrows.

Front

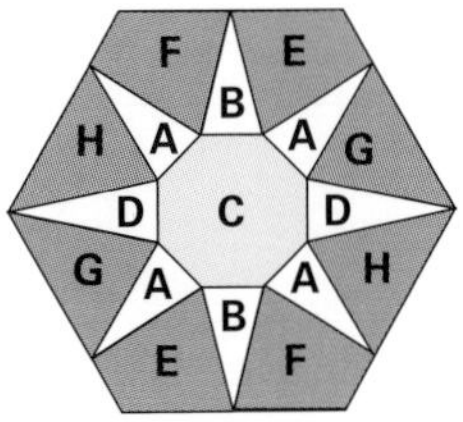

On point

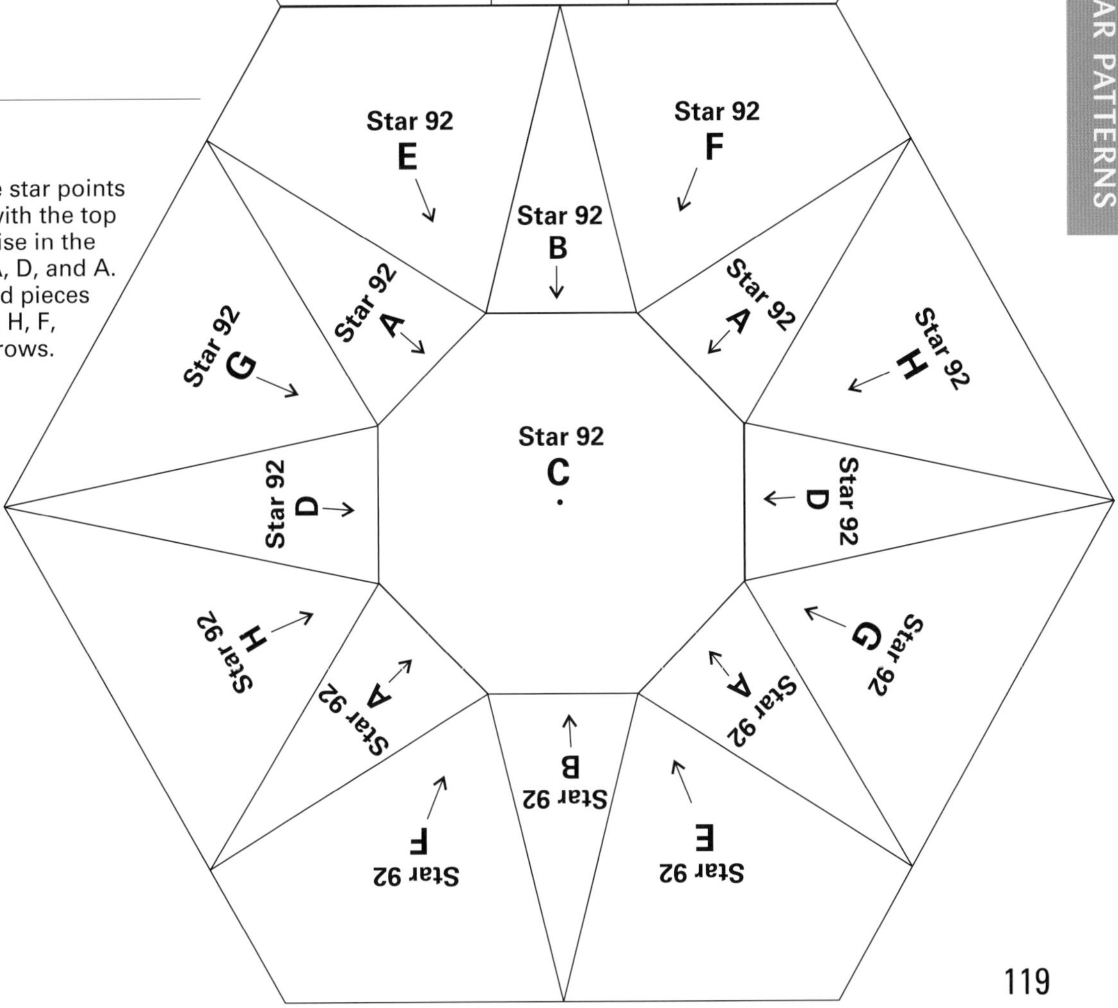

Star 91 G
Star 91 F
Star 91 A
Star 91 B
Star 91 B
Star 91 E
Star 91 D
Star 91 A →
Star 91 C
← A Star 91
Star 91 D
Star 91 B
Star 91 B
Star 91 E
Star 91 A
Star 91 F
Star 91 G

Star 92 E
Star 92 F
Star 92 B
Star 92 G
Star 92 A
Star 92 A
Star 92 H
Star 92 D →
Star 92 C
← D Star 92
Star 92 H
Star 92 A
Star 92 A
Star 92 G
Star 92 B
Star 92 F
Star 92 E

119

Star 93

Focus on the six triangular wedges: join A pieces to B pieces, and then add C pieces. Lay the finished wedges out as in the diagram (or try different rotations, like the star block below). Stitch the wedges into two groups of three. Join the half-blocks along the midline.

Front

On point

Star 94

This star has the same pieces as Star 93, but they are mirror images, and three of the six wedges are rotated, putting three C pieces in the block's center, alternating with three center A pieces. Stitch each A to a B, and then add a C, to create six wedges.

Front

On point

Star 93 B

Star 93 C

Star 93 C

Star 93 B

Star 93 B

Star 93 A

Star 93 C

Star 93 A

Star 93 A

Star 93 A

Star 93 C

Star 93 A

Star 93 A

Star 93 B

Star 93 B

Star 93 C

Star 93 B

Star 94 A

Star 94 C

Star 94 B

Star 94 B

Star 94 B

Star 94 C

Star 94 A

Star 94 C

Star 94 A

Star 94 B

Star 94 A

Star 78 A

Star 94 C

Star 94 C

Star 94 C

Star 94 A

Star 94 B

Star 94 B

Star 94 A

120

Star 95

The stars on this page have more pieces than Stars 93 and 94, but each is also made up of six triangular wedges that meet in the middle. Each wedge contains an A, B, C, and D. Surround each B with D, C and A, without cutting any thread. Join three ABCD wedges into a half-block, and the other three into the other half. Join the halves. Note: A variation of the mirror image of this block is Star 96, below.

Front

On point

Star 96

This is a variation on the mirror image of Star 95. Surround each B with a C, D, and A. Now there are six triangles. Join three to make one half-block, and three for the other. Join the halves. Option: Instead of C pieces, you can rotate all D or all A pieces to the center—but you can't alternate wedge rotations or the seam allowances may bash into each other!

Front

On point

Star 95 D

Star 95 B

Star 95 C

Star 95 D

Star 95 C

Star 95 B

Star 95 A

Star 95 D

Star 95 B

Star 95 A

Star 95 C

Star 95 A

Star 95 C

Star 95 B

Star 95 A

Star 95 A

Star 95 D

Star 95 C

Star 95 B

Star 95 A

Star 95 B

Star 95 C

Star 95 D

Star 96 D

Star 96 A

Star 96 B

Star 96 A

Star 96 D

Star 96 A

Star 96 B

Star 96 C

Star 96 B

Star 96 D

Star 80 C

Star 96 C

Star 96 A

Star 96 A

Star 96 C

Star 96 B

Star 96 C

Star 96 C

Star 96 D

Star 96 B

Star 80 D

Star 96 D

Star 96 A

Star 96 B

Star 96 A

121

Star 97
E

Star 97
F

Star 97
A

Star 97
B

Star 97
D

Star 97
H

Star 97
G

Star 97
C

Star 97
G

Star 97
D

Star 97
B

Star 97
A

Star 97
H

Star 97
F

Star 97
E

Star 97

Stitch pieces A, B, and D to central piece C. Stitch up the lines between them and then inset pieces E and F. Last, inset pieces G and H.

Front

| F | E |
| G | D | B | A | H |
| C |
| H | A | B | D | G |
| E | F |

On point

Star 98
E

Star 98
F

Star 98
D

Star 98
A

Star 98
B

Star 98
G

Star 98
G

Star 98
D

Star 98
C

Star 98
A

Star 98
E

Star 98
F

Star 98
B

Star 98
A

Star 98
B

Star 98
E

Star 98
D

Star 98
G

Star 98
F

Star 98

Join each E to an A. Join each AE unit to a D. Make three AEDs. Join each B to an F. Add a G to each BF unit. Make three. When surrounding C, start at the 1 o'clock position in the diagram, add wedge AED, GFB, AED, GFB, AED, and GFB. Last, sew the seams between the wedges.

Front

F	E
G	B	A	D
D	G
E	A	C	B	F
B	A
F	G	D	E

On point

Star 99

Sew each A between an E and a B. When surrounding piece C, start at the 12 o'clock position and add F, unit BAE, piece D, F, BAE, and D. Sew the seams that extend out from piece C. Variation: A more complex option will put a square in the block's center. Cut C apart along the dotted lines. Sew the two triangular points to the center square. Treat the entire unit as piece C.

Front

On point

Star 100

Join piece A to B. Sew that unit to G. Join piece H to I. Sew that unit to piece M. Surround piece C in this order: Clockwise from the top, attach piece D, unit BAG, E, K, MIH, J. Last, inset pieces F and L. Variation: Cut piece C on the dotted lines. In that case, sew the triangular points to the central square of C. Then treat the entire unit as one piece.

Front

On point

Star 99 D

Star 99 E

Star 99 F

Star 99 B

Star 99 A

Star 99 C

Star 99 A

Star 99 B

Star 99 F

Star 99 E

Star 99 D

Star 100 J

Star 100 H

Star 100 I

Star 100 D

Star 100 B

Star 100 A

Star 100 C

Star 100 M

Star 100 L

Star 100 G

Star 100 K

Star 100 F

Star 100 E

123

Star 101
F

Star 101
G

Star 101
B

Star 101
A

Star 101
H

Star 101
I

Star 101
A

Star 101
E

Star 101
C
•

Star 101
E

Star 101
A

Star 101
A

Star 101
I

Star 101
H

Star 101
B

Star 101
G

Star 101
F

Star 101

Join one A to one G. Repeat with a second A to a G. Join a third A to a piece I. Join the final A to an I. Join each E to an H. Attach all of the units to the central square: starting at the 12 o'clock position, attach BF, AI, EH, AG, BF, AI, EH, and AG. Stitch the seams that emanate from piece C.

Front

G F
H A B
E A I
I A E
B A H
F G

On point

Star 102
F

Star 102
G

Star 102
B

Star 102
E

Star 102
A

Star 102
D

Star 102
H

Star 102
C
•

Star 102
H

Star 102
D

Star 102
A

Star 102
E

Star 102
B

Star 102
G

Star 102
F

Star 102

Join each A to an E. Join each B to an F. Surround square C with adjoining pieces: referring to the diagram and starting in the 12 o'clock position, attach BF, AE, D, BF, AE, and D to C. Inset G and H on either side of the D pieces. Stitch up the seams, emanating from the center.

Front

G F
H D B A
E A C D H
B D G
F

On point

Star 103

Join each A to a B. Referring to the diagram, stitch the upper left AB unit along the left side of triangle C (you can't sew all the way up piece B). Moving counterclockwise, join another AB unit alongside the bottom of piece C (and the first A). Sew the final BA unit in position to the right. Stitch the remaining seams.

Front

On point

Star 104

Join each A to a B. Referring to the diagram, stitch one BA unit to the left side of triangle C. Moving counterclockwise, join another BA unit to the bottom of pieces A and C. Finally, add the third BA unit to the right side of triangle C. Stitch the remaining seams.

Front

On point

Star 103 **A**

Star 103 **B**

Star 103 **A**

Star 103 **C** .

Star 103 **B**

Star 103 **A**

Star 103 **B**

Star 104 **A**

Star 104 **B**

Star 104 **A**

Star 104 **C** .

Star 104 **B**

Star 104 **B**

Star 104 **A**

125

Star 105
Sew each A between an E and a D piece. Stitch the DAE units surrounding the central C triangle. Inset the B pieces.

Star 105
B

Star 105
D

Star 105
E

Star 105
A

Star 105
E

Star 105
C

Star 105
D

Star 105
B

Star 105
D

Star 105
A

Star 105
E

Star 105
B

Front

On point

Star 106
Sew each A between an E and a D piece. Sew each DAE unit to each side of triangle C. Inset the B pieces.

Star 106
B

Star 106
D

Star 106
E

Star 106
A

Star 106
A

Star 106
C

Star 106
E

Star 106
D

Star 106
B

Star 106
D

Star 106
A

Star 106
E

Star 106
B

Front

On point

Star 107

Referring to the diagram, stitch each B on top of each A. Add each C to the left of each AB. Join three ABC triangles together. Join the three remaining ABC triangles together. Join the halves.

Front

On point

Star 108

Join each A to a B. Join three AB triangles together. Join the remaining AB triangles together. Join the halves.

Front

On point

Star 107 B
Star 107 C
Star 107 B
Star 107 C
Star 107 B
Star 107 A
Star 107 A
Star 107 C
Star 107 A
Star 107 C
Star 107 B
Star 107 A
Star 107 A
Star 107 B
Star 107 C
Star 107 B
Star 107 C

Star 108 B
Star 108 A
Star 108 B
Star 108 A
Star 108 B
Star 108 A
Star 108 A
Star 108 B
Star 108 A
Star 108 B

Star 109
F

Star 109
A

Star 109
K

Star 109
D

Star 109
B

Star 109
G

Star 109
C

Star 109
J

Star 109
D

Star 109
B

Star 109
H

Star 109
E

Star 109
I

Star 109

Working clockwise in the front diagram, surround C with pieces A, D, D, E, B, and B, in order. Inset pieces F, G, H, I, J, and K, making sure you're placing them between the correct star points.

Front

K A F
J B C D G
B D
I E H

On point

Star 110
F

Star 110
A

Star 110
B

Star 110
C

Star 110
G

Star 110
D

Star 110
E

Star 110
H

Star 110

Stitch pieces A, B, D, and E to piece C. Inset background pieces F, G, and H, paying close attention to placement.

Front

F A
B C
G
D E
H

On point

Star 111

Construct in three units. First, join D to F. Next, join G to E. Going clockwise around the diagram, sew DF between H and B. Sew GE between I and C. Starting at the broad end of triangle A, sew one side to unit BDFH. Sew the other side to unit CEGI.

Front

I H
G E D F
C A B

On point

Star 111 **H**

Star 111 **I**

Star 111 **F**

Star 111 **D**

Star 111 **E**

Star 111 **G**

Star 111 **A**

Star 111 **B**

Star 111 **C**

Star 112

Join pieces A, B, and D to piece C. Inset F and E.

Front

D F B E
C A

On point

Star 112 **F**

Star 112 **D**

Star 112 **E**

Star 112 **B**

Star 112 **C**

Star 112 **A**

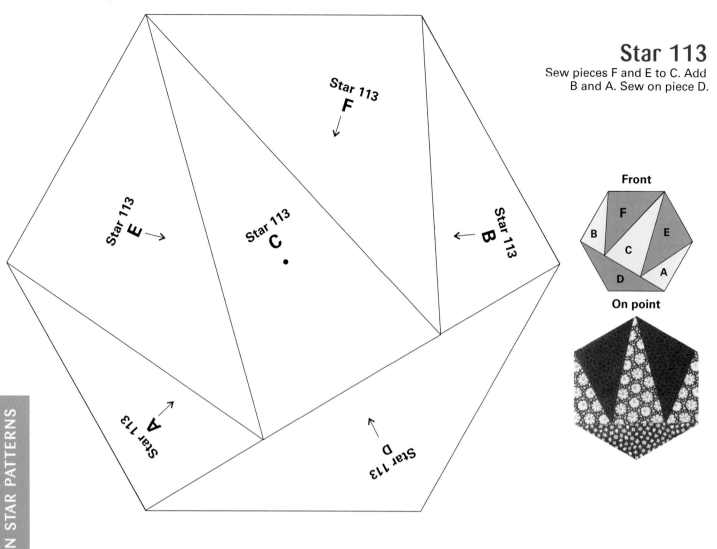

Star 113

Sew pieces F and E to C. Add
B and A. Sew on piece D.

Front

On point

Full-Size Setting Shapes

The grids on the following pages will allow you to photocopy and then cut out several different full-size setting shapes.

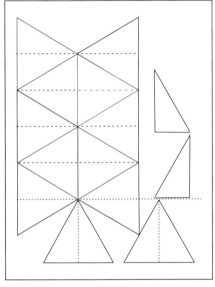

PATTERN 1, page 132

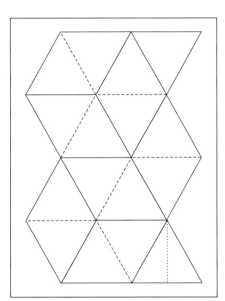

PATTERN 2, page 133

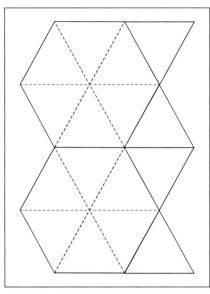

PATTERN 3, page 134

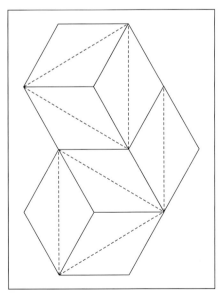

PATTERN 4, page 135

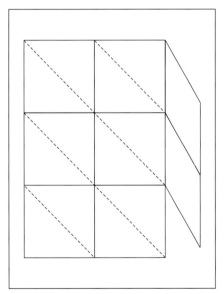

PATTERN 5, page 136

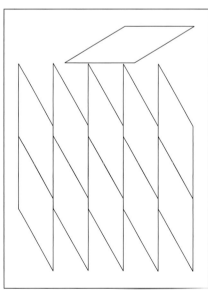

PATTERN 6, page 137

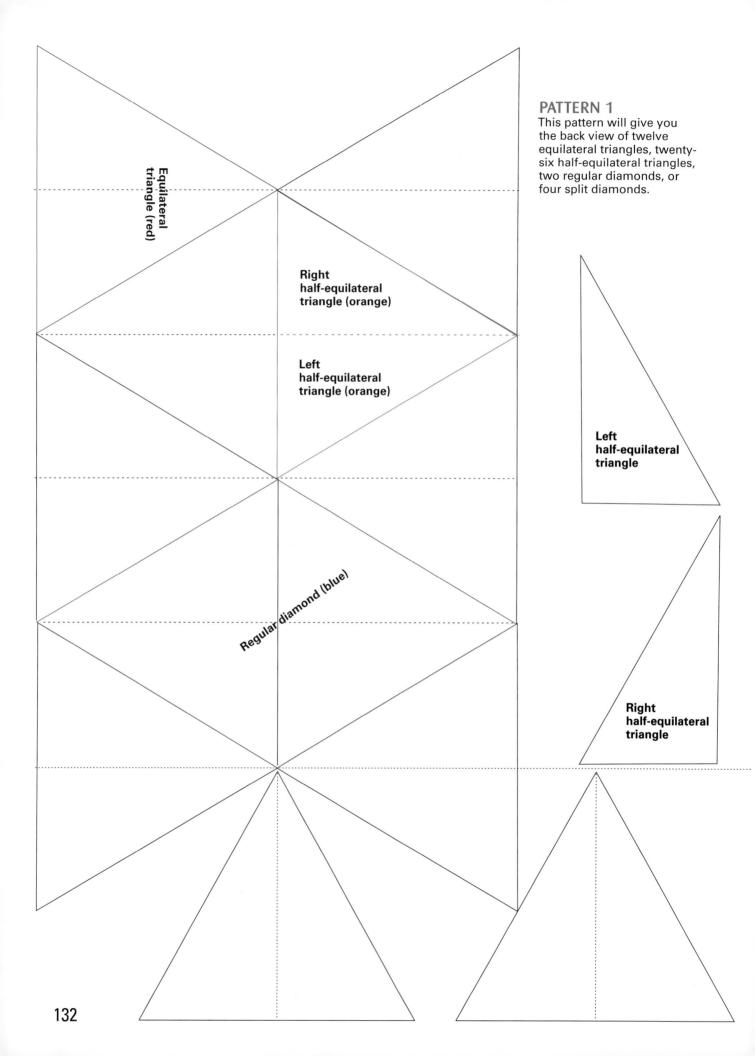

PATTERN 1
This pattern will give you the back view of twelve equilateral triangles, twenty-six half-equilateral triangles, two regular diamonds, or four split diamonds.

Equilateral triangle (red)

Right half-equilateral triangle (orange)

Left half-equilateral triangle (orange)

Regular diamond (blue)

Left half-equilateral triangle

Right half-equilateral triangle

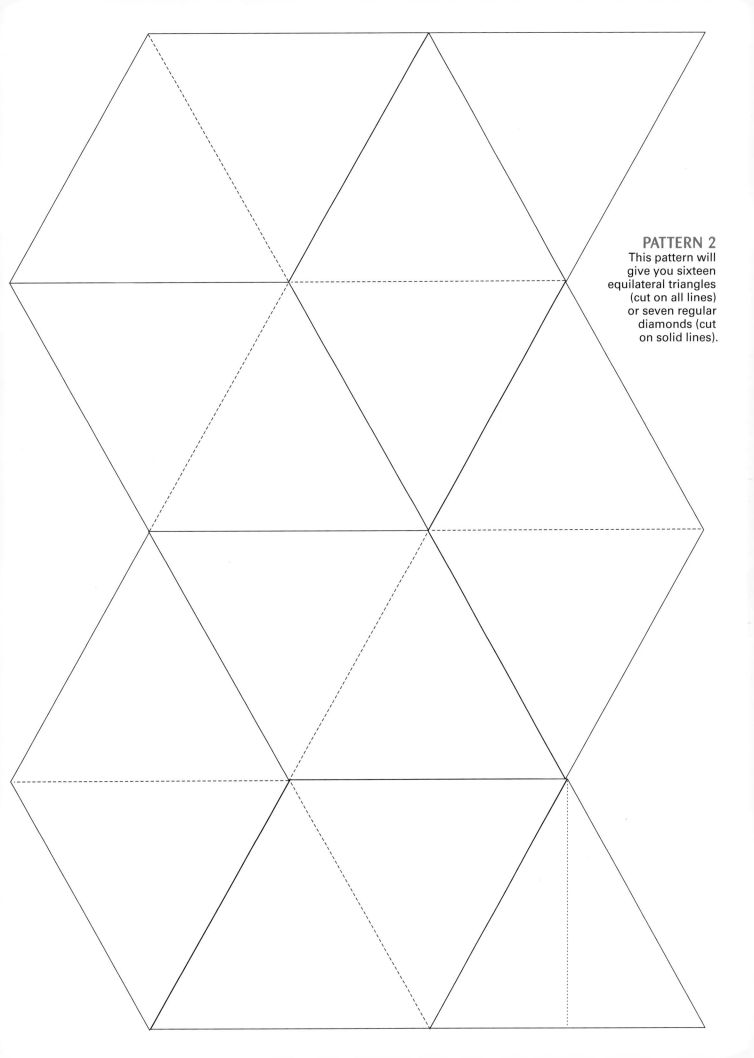

PATTERN 2
This pattern will
give you sixteen
equilateral triangles
(cut on all lines)
or seven regular
diamonds (cut
on solid lines).

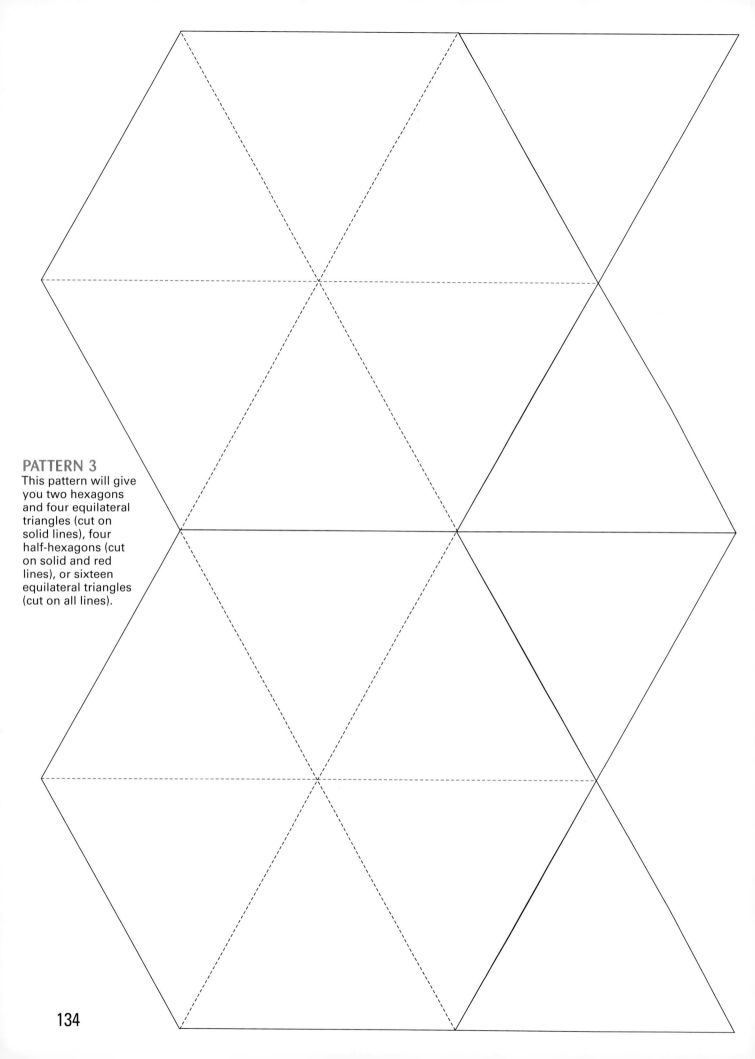

PATTERN 3
This pattern will give you two hexagons and four equilateral triangles (cut on solid lines), four half-hexagons (cut on solid and red lines), or sixteen equilateral triangles (cut on all lines).

134

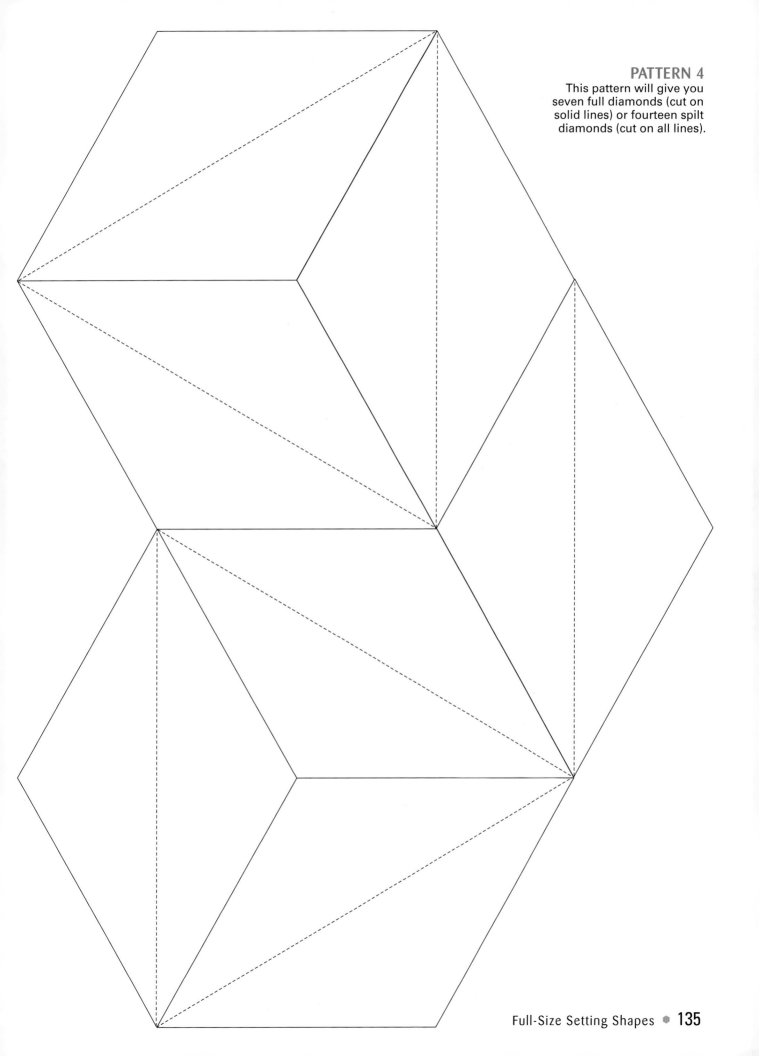

PATTERN 4
This pattern will give you seven full diamonds (cut on solid lines) or fourteen spilt diamonds (cut on all lines).

PATTERN 5

This pattern will give you six squares (cut on solid lines) or twelve half-square triangles (cut on all lines). There are also two narrow diamonds on the far right. Tip: The squares on this page can easily be rotary-cut from cardstock without photocopying. Cut them to 3" x 3" (7.6 x 7.6cm). For the same size half-square triangles as these, rotary-cut the 3" (7.6cm) squares from corner to corner.

PATTERN 6
This pattern will give you eleven
narrow diamonds (cut on all lines).

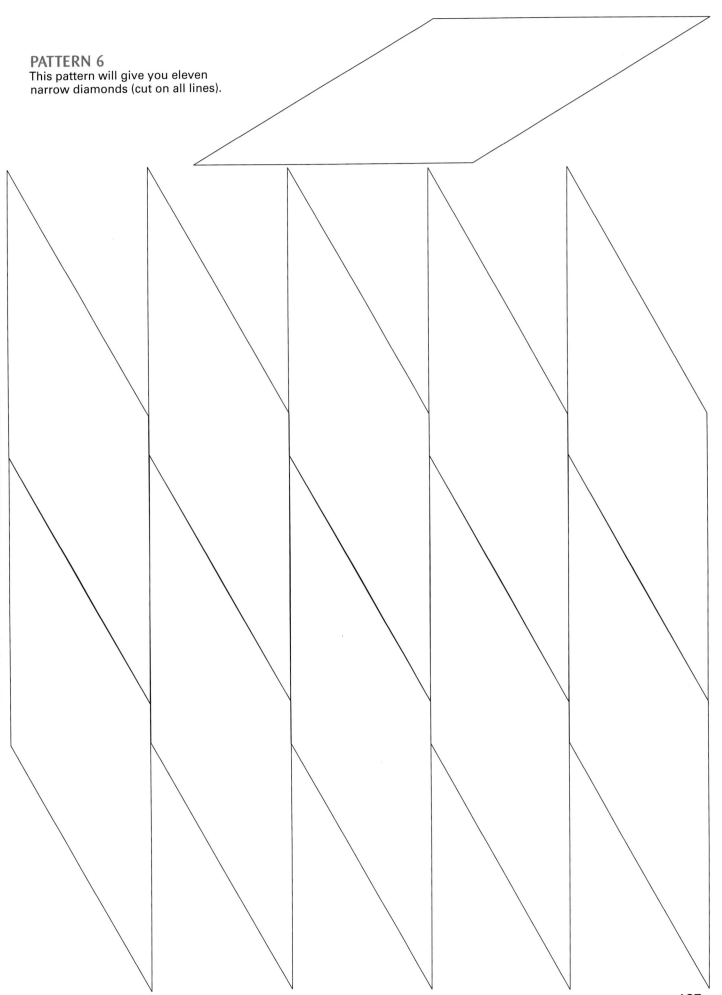

Use Wooden or Paper Blocks

In the early 2000s, when my kids were small, I scored this pail of blocks at a yard sale. There were several different sets jumbled up, and one of them was an assortment of ½" (1.3cm)–thick, brightly colored wooden hexagon-related shapes: hexagons, half-hexagons, squares, equilateral triangles, diamonds that are 60 degrees at their narrow points, and split diamonds that are 30 degrees at their narrow points (A).

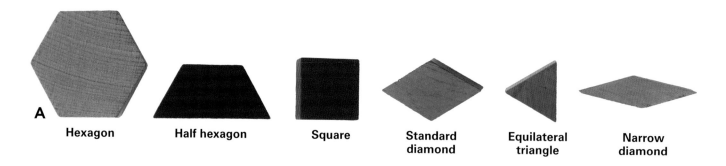

A

| Hexagon | Half hexagon | Square | Standard diamond | Equilateral triangle | Narrow diamond |

My family loved making elaborate formations from them! When we particularly liked a creation, I would take a picture. After the kids moved out, I kept the pail on the back of a sewing-room shelf, knowing that I'd need them again.

While EPPing the stars in this book, and pondering what to do with them, the blocks sprang to mind. I dug out the pail.

Using the yellow hexagons as stand-ins for star blocks, I discovered that it's much more liberating to play with blocks than draw on graph paper or even a computer program. The more pieces you add, the more interesting it gets. Start minimal (B) and keep adding (C, D). The design goes from nice to POW (E)!

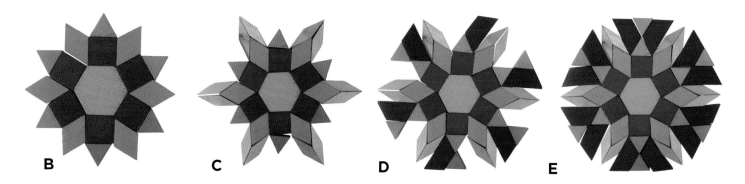

B   **C**   **D**   **E**

You too can play with these blocks, or a reasonable facsimile. I found sets of blocks like these online by School Smart®. They're called Wooden Pattern Blocks, and they're inexpensive!

If you don't feel like buying the blocks, you can simply use the color-and-cut play shapes on pages 141–142. The sizes on those pages match up with all of the little gray-scale diagrams next to each star pattern in this book; each tiny hexagon is 1½" (3.8cm) across at its widest.

After you finish making each star, cut out the gray-scale diagram and save the diagrams in a plastic bag or envelope. You can then conduct your own play sessions, along with the small shapes (color them if you like!). This is also a good way to partner up with a child (or spouse or neighbor) who doesn't sew—ask the person to arrange the blocks, and you stitch it up.

ADDITIONAL SHAPES

Along with the original toy block shapes, I've added FOUR more for this book: a half-square triangle (F), a split diamond (G), and two equilateral triangle halves, the left (H) and the right halves (I).

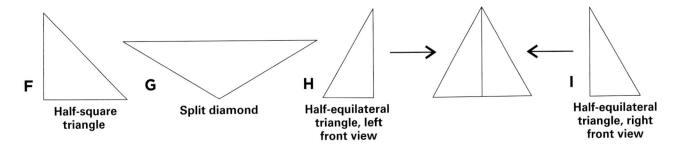

F Half-square triangle

G Split diamond

H Half-equilateral triangle, left front view

I Half-equilateral triangle, right front view

Finished formations are fairly easy to appliqué to a background using a process that's basically needle-turn appliqué. (See pages 36–38.)

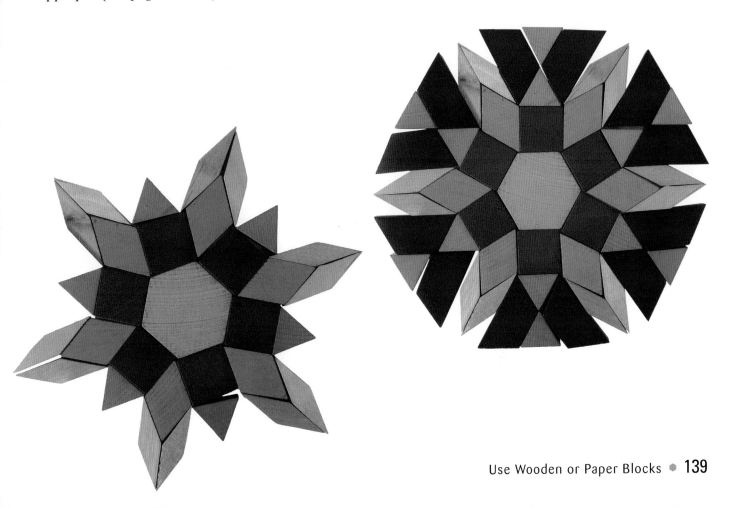

Brainstorming Layouts

The star blocks are gray in these sample layouts. These formations can serve as a launching pad for your creations.

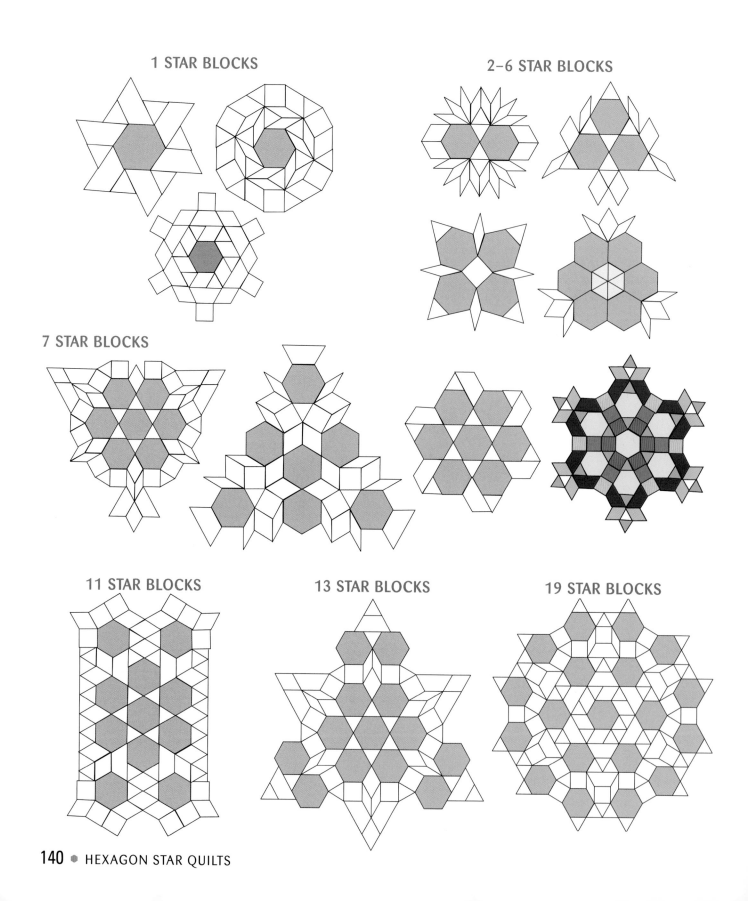

1 STAR BLOCKS

2–6 STAR BLOCKS

7 STAR BLOCKS

11 STAR BLOCKS

13 STAR BLOCKS

19 STAR BLOCKS

Copy, Cut, Color, and Play Shapes

You can buy an inexpensive set of hexagon-related blocks to play with, or you can just use the shapes on these pages. Cut out each star diagram after you finish the star. The diagrams are 1½" (3.8cm) across at their widest point. Each side is ¾" (1.9cm). All these setting shapes have ¾" (1.9cm) sides. You may want to use crayons or markers to color these shapes. You can also cut out the photos to include, but their sizes aren't as regular as the diagrams.

HEXAGONS FOR PLAYING
Cut on solid lines for hexagons, equilateral triangles, and diamonds (two equilateral triangles with bases together, uncut). Cut on dotted lines for half-hexagons, half-equilateral triangles, and split diamonds. Color as desired.

NARROW TRIANGLES FOR PLAYING

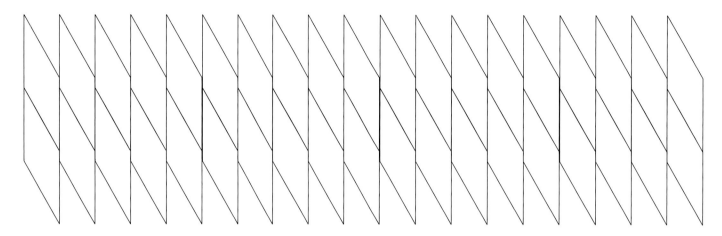

SQUARES/HALF-SQUARE TRIANGLES FOR PLAYING
Cut on solid lines for squares and cut on dotted lines for half-square triangles.

EXTRA BLOCKS FOR PLAYING
Cut around the perimeter for hexagons, and then down the dotted line on each for half-hexagons. Cut along all lines for triangles.

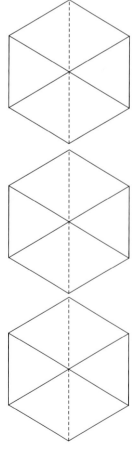

Index

Note: Page numbers in *italics* indicate projects.

About the Author

CATHY PERLMUTTER is a fiber artist, teacher, writer, and editor living in southern California. Her quilts have appeared in many shows, including International Quilt Festival Houston, Road to California, and QuiltCon. See more of her quilts and learn about her online classes at her website, *cathyperlmutter.com*. She sells patterns for quilts and other stitched objects–ranging from English Paper Pieced polyhedrons to improvisational stuffed animals–at her Etsy shop, *www.etsy.com/shop/ CathyPStudio*.

PHOTO BY MARIAN SUNABE

PHOTO CREDITS
Images from *www.Shutterstock.com*: Andrey Eremin (top right 9); Tada Images (left 9); Kabardin's photo (top left 10); megaflopp (top left 10); PolinaPersikova (bottom 10); pelfophoto (top right 11); Anton Starikov (bottom 11).